SEXUAL ASSAUL
The Dilemma of D

'92

SEXUAL ASSAULT:

THE DILEMMA OF DISCLOSURE, THE QUESTION OF CONVICTION

Rita Gunn
Candice Minch

UNIVERSITY OF MANITOBA PRESS

Design: Norman Schmidt
Printed in Canada

Dedicated to all those who have suffered the
degradation and violence of sexual assault.
Your courage is an inspiration that change is
possible.

The Outreach Fund of the University
of Manitoba has assisted us in the
distribution of this book.

Canadian Cataloguing in Publication Data

Gunn, Rita F.

Sexual assault

Includes bibliographical references and index.
ISBN 0-88755-144-0 (bound) - 0-88755-618-3 (pbk.)

1. Sex crimes - Canada. 2. Rape - Canada.
I. Minch, Candice P. II. Title.

KE8928.G86 1988 364.1'53'0971 C88-098096-6

CONTENTS

INTRODUCTION

Sexual assault enforces a restricted lifestyle on *all* women. The ever-conscious threat of an attack limits the behaviour and activities of females throughout their lives. Moreover, the actual occurrence of a sexual assault begins a process that does not end with the attack itself. The victim must face more than her own personal trauma in response to the event. She must decide whether and to whom she will disclose the incident. If she chooses to inform the police, she may be victimized again by the legal system.

Sexual assault is a criminal offence and, as for all criminal offences, an alleged offender is innocent until proven guilty. The legislation on sexual assault, however, is unique in its emphasis on consent and the character of the victim. Unlike most other offences, then, the victim of a sexual assault may feel that she is guilty until proven innocent. Consequently, in deciding whether to officially report an assault, the victim is caught in a dilemma. If she chooses not to report the assault, the offender goes unchallenged. If she chooses to report, she may be subjected to a legal process that has traditionally displayed skepticism toward females who report sexual assaults.

This book examines the anticipated and actual experiences of the sexual assault victim on both a personal and official level. We focus on the reactions of significant others (family, friends) and the criminal justice system (police, prosecution, courts) to the offence. The response by others is crucial, as it defines the event to the victim and ultimately to society.

The book is based on research undertaken in two separate studies, both of which confront systemic prejudices against women who have been sexually assaulted. The first study delves into the victim's perspective and exposes the internalized guilt that women endure when they have been victimized. The second scrutinizes the legal process and the inequities inherent in the system.

In research with victims we assess what led them to report a sexual assault to the police or to refrain from doing so. Other researchers (for example, Amir 1971) have identified possible contributing factors with the use of statistical data, but victim surveys have not systematically studied specific criteria. We isolated and tested several variables by gaining access to a crisis centre, an agency that provides victims with an alternative method of "unofficially" reporting sexual offences. Although crisis centres offer services to women who do report their victimization officially to the police, many of their clients choose not to become involved with the criminal justice system. Interviewing victims at such a facility provides first-hand information about women's perceptions of their assaults. With the results of these interviews, specific variables are correlated with individual decisions regarding disclosure of the incidents.

Our research at the criminal justice level reveals how the legal system deals with sexual assault. While the majority of research on sexual assault has concentrated on police-level processing (for example, Clark and Lewis 1977), we study the filtering system of the reports at the police, crown attorney, and court levels in order to examine the entire system. We also focus on the role of the prosecutor in sexual assault proceedings as the crucial link between the police and court levels. While crown attorneys have an obvious direct influence over charges in the court system, they also have an influence on police proceedings, albeit in a less direct manner. The police must make decisions on charges based on their expectations of the crown's willingness to accept and proceed with the charges in the court system.

At this level we deal with the legal offences of rape and attempted rape which were in effect at the time of the research. These data were collected prior to the enactment of the new sexual assault legislation which came into effect in January 1983. The new legislation replaces the former offences of rape, attempted rape and indecent assault with a three-tiered classification of sexual assault based on the degree of violence. Under the old law, if there was no vaginal penetration by a penis, a rape charge could not be laid.

Our intent was to examine the filtering system of sexual offences which were classified and handled as such by the criminal justice system. Obviously, the only way to achieve this was to obtain access to official police records. However, other offences, although sexual in nature, might not have been dealt with as sexual offences under the old legislation because of the extreme discretionary powers of the police and the limiting definitions under the old legislation. Consequently, to gather a sufficient number of cases with which to obtain detailed information for the following through of charges from the police level to final disposition, it became necessary to use the data that were available from an official source. We have utilized the broader term of sexual assault in the text of the monograph. Any reference to rape will relate to other studies cited prior to 1983 or where the former definition was associated with charges proceeding through the criminal justice system.

At the level of the victim, restricting ourselves to a legal definition of rape would have put severe limitations on the data that were available to us. The nature of the agency where the research was conducted allowed us access to victims of every type of sexual assault. Thus, it was possible to acquire a broad representation of all forms of sexual offences, irrespective of any legal definition. For this portion of the research, sexual assault has been defined as any sexual act perpetrated on a female against her will by means of physical force, intimidation, blackmail or authority.

The remainder of our discussion will be organized as follows: Chapter 1 describes the social context in which sexual assault occurs. Here it will be suggested that the occurrence of sexual assault can best be understood by viewing it in the context of a patriarchal society, where male aggression is fostered. Chapter 2 addresses the extent of under-reporting by sexual assault victims and the resulting myths and stereotypes that are perpetuated by the press and the legal system. Chapter 3 discusses the effects of socialization, including double standards of sexual behaviour, violence toward females and the resulting personal and legal responses. Chapters 4, 5 and 6 contain our research. Chapter 4 deals with the victim's response to sexual assault while chapters 5 and 6 address the response of the legal system and the role of the prosecutor, respectively. In chapter 7, we discuss the major features of the new sexual assault legislation and provide a preliminary analysis of the handling of sexual assault charges. Chapter 8 provides a synthesis of our research findings and ideas on the direction needed in further addressing the problem of sexual assault.

We undertook the writing this book with the intention of reaching a wide and diverse audience. It was important to us that the experience and knowledge we acquired as a result of our research would not sit on a shelf covered with a film of dust, retrieved occasionally, and purely for academic purposes. As such, we hope it will be read by students studying in the social sciences, sexual assault victims, those who counsel and provide support to victims, and the general public. To those who shared their experiences with us, this is a recognition of their courage and we hope they approve of our understanding and articulation of the dilemmas encountered by sexual assault victims.

SEXUAL ASSAULT:
The Dilemma of Disclosure, The Question of Conviction

CHAPTER I

The Social Context of Sexual Assault

THE widespread belief that women have made great strides toward equality with men is epitomized by the commercial cliché, "You've come a long way, baby!" It is a popular misconception that women have attained full freedom of choice and that authentic equality, based on ability and ambition, exists. Men are still at the helm of our economic, political, legal and religious institutions, making decisions that affect the lives of women.

The success of the women's movement in effecting social change through political pressure has been limited. Although advances have been made in the social, political and economic spheres, these changes have had little effect on the day-to-day lives of most women. The theoretical perspective that has guided and informed our inquiry on sexual assault focuses on the concept of "patriarchy" and its implications. Patriarchy refers to a gender-based differentiation of roles which becomes defined as a "natural" right of males to make decisions and monopolize positions of authority in society and its dominant institutions. This is not so much a deliberate, conscious effort on the part of males to control as it is a historically bound phenomenon in which women have been viewed as the property of men. Implicit in the concept of patriarchy is the notion of the power of males over females. If there is consensus in the assumption that sexual assault is a violent act involving power and dominance, then we must

look at the differences in power between men and women
in society.

The notion that women have achieved equal status in
relation to men is contradicted by their continued subor-
dination in virtually all spheres of social life. Men are still
making the decisions that control the lives and the consciousness of women.

An important part of this reality and, hence, a real
limitation is that women continue to occupy the traditional, low-paying, female-dominated occupations; that is,
women's jobs are concentrated in the areas of sales,
teaching, service, health and clerical work. In fact, their
participation rate in these occupations rose from 71 percent in 1971 to 74 percent in 1981 (Statistics Canada
1984). The federal minister responsible for the status of
women reported in 1986 that the wage gap between men
and women for full-time work has persisted.

According to a 1987 Statistics Canada report, women
currently earn 66 cents for every dollar earned by men,
only a slight improvement over the 58 cents for every dollar figure they earned in 1967. This translates into
average full-time salaries of $19,000 for women and
$30,131 for men. Education is found to reduce the dif-
ferential in wages, with a university degree resulting in
women earning 19 percent less than their male counter-
parts. Although education may reduce the disparity
somewhat, women in general continue to earn less than
men.

Most part-time workers are women. Among the
1,477,000 part-time workers (13.5 percent of all workers)
in the Canadian labour force in 1985, 71 percent were
women. In general, part-time workers receive fewer
benefits in terms of pensions, unionization, and job

security and are paid less than full-time employees, even
where there is no disparity in educational levels. While
one-fifth of all part-time workers would prefer full-time
employment, 70 percent of these dissatisfied workers are
female (CACSW 1985a). Yet attitudes persist that women
are taking jobs away from men and that this is a crucial
factor in the Canadian unemployment situation. In fact,
unemployment rates are consistently higher for women
than men (NCW 1985).

These circumstances persist, in large part, because of
the belief that women are secondary earners who are
working, not out of economic necessity, but because of a
so-called "boredom" with their domestic role. This idea,
reinforced by the belief that the foremost obligation of
women is within the domestic sphere, causes working
women an enormous amount of self-doubt and guilt. If
they have children, they bear the additional burden of
being accused of maternal neglect. Delinquency is seldom
attributed to working fathers. A Senate Committee report,
"Child at Risk," claims that "maternal deprivation has a
detrimental effect on character development" (1980, 33).
It is a wretched double bind for women when nearly 61
percent of Canadian families would be living below the
poverty line if wives and mothers were not contributing to
the household income (CACSW 1985b). At the same time,
although more men are claiming to be involved in
household tasks, their participation remains relatively
small. In a Gallup Poll taken in 1981, there was no significant change in the distribution of housework from an
earlier poll taken in 1958 (Boyd 1984). Thus, while more
women are required to work outside the home to supple-
ment the family income, societal expectations still dictate

that they retain the major responsibilities within the home.

These adversities are accompanied by the fact that most of the people who live at or below the poverty level are women. In 1984, according to a survey of Canadians by the National Council on Welfare, 43 percent of single women were found to be poor in contrast to 32 percent of single men. The gap widens with families headed by a female or male parent. Here, poverty levels for women are at 43 percent compared to those for men at 11 percent. The report describes Canada's elderly women as the most poverty stricken: 80 percent of women over the age of 65 are poor, compared to 29 percent of men (NCW 1985).

In political life, women are still found in the "housekeeping" tasks. With few exceptions, they participate in party organization and support functions at the citizen level, as opposed to acquiring true political authority. In 1983, for example, out of 1,018 members in federal and provincial politics, there were only 67 women, a representation of 6.6 percent. Federally, in the spring of 1988, they occupied 29 out of 282 seats in the House of Commons, with no representation from Manitoba, Saskatchewan, the Northwest Territories or the Atlantic provinces. This is clearly inadequate, as women constitute slightly over one-half of Canada's population. As a result, women retain minority status and have minimal input into the passing of laws, while men make the decisions that control the lives of women as well as their own.

Those women who do penetrate the male domain of politics and are elected members of government are often fielded into the area with the least power and status – the back-benches of government. Here women have little power, and primarily serve to raise regional or local concerns and to support the positions and decisions taken by the party's hierarchy. Positions of power in government are rarely accorded to women, whose portfolios usually include those that are less desirable and therefore less sought after by men. A few women who have achieved some measure of political status have complained that voicing concern for women's issues causes them to be labelled "radical feminists" and results in the tendency for male colleagues to dismiss their opinions on that basis. This is the sort of disparagement that women find defeating and frustrating when they rise to a position of some power. The quandary they face is how to maintain political effectiveness in establishing rights for women and still retain the respect of male colleagues who are less concerned with human issues when they relate to women. Until female representation in politics is increased and there is a corresponding sensitivity to the rights and needs of women, there will continue to be little concern for realizing real equality and enshrining it in the law.

While parliament legislates, the laws are interpreted and applied by the legal profession. This has traditionally meant that laws made by men have been interpreted and applied by men. It appears that women are advancing in this institution, as shown by law school enrollments and bar admissions which indicate that more women are pursuing law degrees. But these gains are not found among practising lawyers. Statistics obtained from the provincial law societies list 7,049 women out of a total of 46,036 practising lawyers in Canada, as of July 1985 (Manitoba Bar Assn. 1986). This translates into female representation of only 15 percent in the legal profession.

The low status of women lawyers is reflected in an analysis of their placement within the legal hierarchy. At the top of the pyramid are judges, the large majority of whom are male. In 1979 there were 18 federally appointed female superior court judges out of a total of 630 in Canadian courtrooms (CACSW 1979). In 1985, female federal appointees rose from 18 to 28, a 36 percent increase in six years, but still only an insignificant proportion overall (Egan 1985). A 1982 survey of provincial judges in Canada (except Quebec which did not provide data) shows 22 women out of a total of 572 in the six provinces with at least minimal female representation (Zwarun 1985). As of 1988 there have been three women appointed to the Manitoba Court of Queen's Bench, with two assigned to the Family Division. A woman's place, even in the courtroom, is found to be in the realm of the family. Women's nature is assumed to be intrinsically bound up with domestic life and the courtroom is no exception. Of a total of 77 Manitoba judges in spring 1988, there were 6 women.

It is evident from the above data that women are still largely excluded from the major roles outside the home, relegated to domestic life and the responsibilities associated with the family. There is no denying that these duties are honourable and essential, but little status is bestowed upon those who perform them. Patriarchy does not provide choices. A society that places a high value on economic reward and achievement does not allow freedom to decide one's role. Free choice is illusionary when social expectations and social structure designate roles. Competition for high status and lucrative positions is limited to persons (mainly male) who can afford the time and dedication that is demanded of them. We are aware of the rising number of "superwomen" who manage, albeit with guilt, stress and exhaustion, both family and career. But major advances in the economic and political spheres cannot be achieved with a half-time commitment. It is apparent that men have had the freedom to pursue power and claim access to most of the resources that perpetuate their power, because of a notable biological difference: they cannot give birth to children! While the dictionary defines the term parent as a mother or father, parenting is mainly performed by the child-bearer – the mother.

Although child-bearing is a biological fact associated with women, the assignment of child-rearing has been socially designated to females. One of the major ways in which patriarchy is perpetuated is through the existence of the traditional nuclear family, consisting of a father, mother and children. The role of the female as wife and mother within this framework involves the provision of domestic labour and sexual services, as well as the reproduction and care of children. These services are provided for men and are controlled by men. This work differs substantially from paid male labour in the public sphere, as women provide these services for social, not financial, rewards. Male control of women's labour (production/reproduction) enhances their dominant position and maintains women in a dependent role.

The preparation of the sexes for their respective roles in a society dominated by a male power structure is accomplished through gender-based socialization. The most reliable predictor of future behaviour is likely the assignment of gender at birth. It is the categorization of expectations that accompany being "male" or "female" that will define the path of the socialized person. In general, females are encouraged to be nurturing, deferring and dependent, while males are taught to be aggressive, strong and independent. Such pre-defined behavioural traits become a blueprint for what is considered "normal" behaviour. Males and females are treated differently, are subject to differing expectations, and get rewarded for responding appropriately. That is the way the world unfolds for each human as they learn the norms of society. In this way, our reality and our world are socially constructed and we learn to interpret our experiences according to a prescribed frame of reference.

One of the obvious vehicles for perpetuating the prevalent image of males and females is the media. Given the pervasiveness of its influence, the media plays a crucial role in socialization. Sex-role stereotyping is actually a technique which is purposely used by advertisers in the media to create an idealized image of reality (Supply and Services Canada 1982). Not only are adults having their harmful and inaccurate beliefs validated, but children are being indoctrinated and absorbed into patriarchal society. Relatively few attempts have been made to reverse roles and balance the portrayal of males and females and these have been insufficient to ward off the cumulative effects of yet another male-dominated institution.

The roles we enact, then, are socially created and reflect accepted patterns of behaviour in society. For example, in Canadian society, as in others, it is appropriate for females to defer to males. This "norm" is supported by the social structure through, for example, the family and the legal system, so that learning through interaction in society is supported and perpetuated by its institutions.

Organized religion, another major social institution, offers a system of beliefs and values irreconcilable with the principle of women's equality. Therefore changes to improve the status of women are inhibited by religious beliefs which are culturally bound and only applicable to the historical context of their origin. Portrayal of the deity as male and the ideology of male supremacy in the nuclear family perpetuates restrictive gender roles. This is not surprising, since religious laws, like secular laws, have been written, interpreted and primarily enforced by men. This can be seen in the way that churches still retain control over women's bodies with women often having little or no voice in matters pertaining to birth control and abortion.

We have provided an examination of institutions and the power base in society in an attempt to understand the social context in which sexual assault occurs. Institutional inequality and rigid roles based on gender maintain and perpetuate the inferior status of females. The traditional definition of female behaviour as subordinate has been strengthened by the training we give our female children to be passive and nurturant. Male superiority, on the other hand, has been enhanced by the way we train male children to be aggressive and to succeed in the economic and political spheres. This extends to their interpersonal relationships with females. Male sexuality is linked to the role of aggressor and some degree of force or coercion is acceptable; importance is placed on the end result, reaching an objective. There is sufficient evidence now that assures us that sexual assault is not motivated by uncontrollable sexual desire. Sexual assault has been exposed as a violent offence involving power and domination (Brownmiller 1975; Clark and Lewis 1977). Whether females are accosted on the street, harassed in the workplace, or fondled at home by their fathers, there is one common theme – an imbalance of power in which violence is implicit. Sexual exploitation, in any form, exemplifies the vulnerability of females because it involves acts that are primarily directed at females in a male dominated society. As such, it is a method by which males can exert control over females in an extreme form along a continuum of male aggressiveness.

CHAPTER II

Understanding Sexual Assault

THE EXTENT OF THE PROBLEM

ONE of the primary obstacles in viewing sexual assault as a significant social problem has been the absence of accurate information on its occurrence. It is a crime that is grossly under-reported. Since it is clear that statistics do not reflect the actual incidence of the crime, it has been impossible to view the severity and extent of the problem in a realistic light. Our work, which examines incidents reported to a crisis centre as well as to the legal system, supplements official statistics by providing information on assaults that have not necessarily been reported to the police. An examination of the criteria differentiating women who make official reports from those who attempt to deal with the assaults in other ways shows that unreported cases are not necessarily comparable to those reported. As stated by Clark and Lewis, "We cannot hope to have anything like a complete picture of rape until all victims are willing to report the crime" (1977, 41).

A victimization survey of 551 women in Winnipeg revealed that one out of every four females had been sexually victimized at some point in her life (Brickman et al. 1980). If this proportion holds for the rest of the country as well, then just over 3 million Canadian women are, or will be victims of sexual assaults. The victimization survey, while more representative than official statistics, nonetheless is not comprehensive and reflects rates based on the sample used. Moreover, it should not be assumed that all the respondents would admit having been sexually assaulted. For the victim who has never disclosed the incident, it might be easier to deny it happened than to allow the stigma and emotional pain associated with the offence to surface. The result is that the least conservative estimates of sexual assault are probably the most representative in gauging its incidence.

PERPETUATION OF MYTHS BY THE PRESS AND THE LEGAL SYSTEM

There is a double standard of sexual behaviour for males and females which is maintained by popular myths. Females are expected to behave in a "virtuous" manner and are condemned for having sexual desires. Males, on the other hand are perceived as "naturally sexual" and are assumed to be unable to control themselves once they have become aroused. It is a common belief that a woman who has been assaulted may have been the cause of her own victimization by behaving in a "promiscuous" manner – a classic example of "blaming the victim" (see Ryan 1974).

The idea that the sexual revolution of the 1960s and 1970s brought about a change in these attitudes is perhaps the most pervasive myth of all. With the onset of the so-called "new morality" it was believed that women were finally entitled to their sexual freedom. Women were being encouraged to be sexually expressive and free from guilt. These ideas were popularized by the media, but society in general still held fast to the old stereotypes. So while women were trying to become less inhibited, they were still feeling guilty. To this day, there are double standards of sexual freedom for women and men.

The persistence of myths and stereotypes is well illustrated by statements made by the media, police, attorneys and judges. The following account describes a case
which commanded considerable attention from the media
and mobilized a city-wide program to apprehend a
"legitimate" assailant. The view that the victim could in
no way be blameworthy is obvious in the description of
her activity at the time of the assault: "At three in the afternoon, a 22-year-old woman was walking home. She was
pushing her 20-month-old daughter in a stroller and was
on a path...crossing a field.... There was a male walking
behind her. He grabbed her and forced her into some near-
by bushes. He began choking her and forcibly removing
her clothing. The baby began to cry. The mother was
struggling...." (*Winnipeg Free Press* Oct. 1984). In addition, the writer inserts his own opinion as he begins the
article with the comment: "It was mid-afternoon on a
weekday, an unlikely time for an attempted rape." He also
suggests that, "Police found the circumstances of the
daylight attack on a young mother were good reasons for
making it...crime of the week."

This case is a conspicuous contrast to the next report.
Consider the obvious value judgments being made despite
the fact that in both cases a woman has been assaulted.
"At about 2 a.m. Sunday a 20-year-old woman was about
to enter her apartment block when two men approached
her and invited her to a party. She agreed to accompany
them but when they arrived at an apartment she found
there was no party. She attempted to leave twice but accepted a drink from the men...." (*Winnipeg Free Press* Dec.
1984). This story was contained in a single article describing several different sexual assaults, including attacks on
a "deaf woman" and a "61-year-old woman". Of the four

assaults reported, the attack on the 20-year-old woman was deemed the one worthy of embellishment. Emphasizing the fact that the woman accepted an invitation from two strangers at 2:00 a.m. and focussing on her acceptance of a drink suggests to the reader that the victim was deserving of her fate. By blaming the victim, the perpetrators have been relieved of responsibility for their conduct. The previous account of a woman fulfilling the most traditional of roles, along with the imagery of her crying baby conjures up a portrait of a woman deserving of protection. The facts about both cases could have been presented more objectively, without comments on the victims' characteristics and activities.

The use of headlines by the media to attract attention can also serve to reinforce inaccurate views on sexual assault. The relationship between hitchhiking and sexual assault is distorted by a police official's comment that appeared as a newspaper heading: "Three young women learn painful hitchhiking lesson" (*Winnipeg Free Press* July 1982). The suggestion evident in the headline is that the victims suffered the due consequences of their own behaviour.

The attitude of the police to victims of sexual assault has been under attack by feminists and other concerned groups. Victims themselves most often report fear of police (and the courts) as a major reason not to report an assault (Solicitor General 1984, 10). This concern is justified when one considers that the police represent the initial contact with the criminal justice system. The police also have a great deal of discretionary power in deciding to proceed with an investigation; they are the first "judges" of whether or not, in their minds, a real assault took place. A statement made by a senior police officer that "spring fever" was to blame for a recent increase of sexual assaults (*Winnipeg Sun* April 1984) is indicative of the kind of attitude that reinforces harmful stereotypes and discourages women from reporting attacks. The suggestion that because women wear less clothing in spring, they inevitably excite normal unsuspecting males, perpetuates the idea that women provoke men into assaulting them.

Responsibility can be attributed to the police for intimidating victims of sexual assault with inaccurate statements like the following: "police walk a tightrope whenever someone cries rape" and "one in four reports are false" (*Winnipeg Sun* Nov. 1981). The expression "cries rape" has become a familiar cliché, alluding to deceit. The designation of a rape charge as "false" when it does not proceed through to the court and result in conviction is misleading. As our research demonstrates, there are many reasons why a complaint may not be pursued (such as an uncooperative victim or insufficient evidence), although an assault took place. The impression given by such statements is that women tend to lie and are untrustworthy.

Defence lawyers have routinely tried to benefit by drawing upon misconceptions and harmful stereotypes of female sexuality in defending rapists. At a Winnipeg rape trial in 1987 the defence lawyer attempted to undermine the victim's credibility with the following statements: "Your honor has seen many black eyes in the courtroom and does not consider those to be bodily harm. I submit it (the laceration) is even less than that. It's not as if he beat her up." The lawyer further stated that his client had no idea that the woman was a virgin. In another case, defence counsel for a 22-year-old man who assaulted a 13-year-old-girl in the basement of a high school suggested that his client "thought the complainant was some-

one he knew and would not object to his conduct." The
judge, responding with humour at the expense of the victim said, "It is an odd way to say hello" (*Winnipeg Free
Press* May 1982). In another story, a defence lawyer ra-
tionalizes the attack by a 26-year-old on a child of 6 by
suggesting that his client was "sexually immature" (*Winnipeg Free Press* May 1983). Lawyers are notorious for
using questionable tactics in courtrooms. Yet, the distrust
is always directed at the victims.

Nor do crown attorneys resist negative stereotyping
when presenting their cases to juries. The following attack on a woman who aided a motorist stuck in a ditch
outside her home is described with poetic fervor by the
crown attorney. The assault, he said was not "the case of
some healthy, young lass walking brazenly...braless, clad
in tight fitting shorts on a sunny Manitoba morn raising
the passions of some hot-blooded youths. Rather, it involved a housewife playing a Good Samaritan role" (*Winnipeg Free Press* Sept. 1980). Evidently, the jury and judge
were in agreement and the offender was sentenced to
three years imprisonment after a half-day trial for attempted rape. Many perpetrators have been given shorter
sentences for more violent attacks. Should we then as-
sume that young women must walk around in heavy
clothing during the summer in order to avoid sexual assault?

In the next case, note the qualifying adjectives used
by a crown attorney in describing the attempted rape and
beating of a woman: "To assault and attempt to rape an
82-year-old woman who was walking down the street with
a bag of groceries in broad daylight...is a crime of utmost
cowardice" (*Winnipeg Free Press* April 1979). The point to
be made here is that the assault was a crime, but the im-

pact of the statement is due to the age of the victim, the time of day and the victim's activities at the time of the assault.

Judges, who represent the height of legal knowledge and experience, have unfortunately not been exempt from relying on myths and misconceptions in exercising their legal powers in the system. Several comments offered by judges presiding over sexual assault cases are worthy of mention. The *Edmonton Journal* (Feb. 1982) contains two such quotes. The first case involves a 5-year-old female assaulted by her mother's live-in boyfriend. In sentencing the 24-year-old offender to a 90-day work release program, the judge explained: "I am satisfied we have an unusually sexually promiscuous young lady. And he (the defendant) did not know enough to refuse. No way do I believe (the man) initiated sexual contact." Perhaps the judge in question was a proponent of Dr. Spock's world-renowned child care book which warns against seductive females in the 3-to-5-year age range! (See Rush 1980.)

The second case concerns three boys aged 15 to 16 years who received no punishment for a sexual assault other than one of the boys being banned from his school for one year. The judge, in attempting to rationalize his decision on their attack of a 16-year-old female, stated in court: "This community is well-known to be sexually permissive. Too many women go around in provocative clothing. Should we punish a 15- or 16-year-old boy who reacts to it normally?"

Another court case reported in the *Winnipeg Free Press* (Jan. 1984) quotes a judge who sentenced a 20-year-old man to four years in prison for the rape of a 33-year-old woman: "One a scale of one to 10, I'd rate this about a two." The victim happened to be an exotic dancer on her way home from work. The crown attorney in objecting to the judge's assessment of the offence retorted in similar vein, using a rating scale: "It should be a seven or eight."

More recently a judge sentenced a 22-year-old offender to a 90-day jail term for the beating and sexual assault of a 27-year-old victim. The offender was allowed to serve his time on weekends. The judge rationalized the sentence by saying that the offender was from a good family and had learned his lesson. He further suggested that there was "no evidence of lasting emotional or psychological harm" even though it took two weeks for the victim to recover from bruises and cuts to her face (*Winnipeg Free Press* Jan. 1988). The judge clearly failed to understand the longer lasting emotional trauma.

THE VICTIM'S INTERNALIZATION OF GUILT
The under-representation of particular kinds of sexual assault in official statistics has also brought about a misunderstanding of the problem for the victim herself. Because of the prevalence of stereotypes, even victims may be unable to define an offence. The belief that only young, attractive, and perhaps careless females are assaulted causes them to define themselves within this context (because nice girls don't get raped). This contradicts the real facts about the offence. Small babies and elderly women are also victims of sexual assaults. Married women are attacked by their husbands and young girls are sexually abused by their fathers. The socialization of women is so powerful that regardless of circumstances, self-blame is inevitable. It should be mentioned here that no value judgment is being made regarding the comparative seriousness of assaults. Socializing at bars and hitch-

ing rides are activities engaged in by both men and women for purposes of recreation and transportation, respectively. Women who are sexually assaulted in those situations should not be accused of "asking for it."

LACK OF IMPETUS BY THE LEGAL SYSTEM

Clearly, the most harmful aspect of the under-reporting of sexual assault has been that we know little about those assaults which are not reported. This has two consequences: the perpetuation of assaults which are perceived to be "legitimate" and are the ones usually reported; and a lack of impetus by the criminal justice system to view sexual assault as a significant social problem meriting legal action. Conventional notions regarding male and female sexuality are extended to sexual assault offences. This results in a harrowing experience for all victims, even those females who are perceived as faultless, when attempting to gain redress through the legal system.

The low number of reported assaults conceals the actual nature of the offence on both a personal and institutional level. A vicious circle emerges whereby the stereotypes of "legitimate" victims and assaults are upheld by society and the legal system. The victim responds in kind by experiencing shame, guilt and fear, and this response limits use of the legal system as a means of justice for the offence committed.

CHAPTER III

The Effects of
Socialization

WOMEN AS OBJECTS OF SEXUAL ENTERTAINMENT

IN a society where women can be bought on the street or viewed in pornographic magazines and films (bound, beaten and mutilated) for the enjoyment of men, a belief system has developed which says that this is how females should be treated. The image of the unwilling woman who is overpowered by a passionate man is a popular movie theme and one which provides implicit cultural approval for this type of sexual interaction. The impression derived from this aggressive–passive form of behaviour is that women want (or need) to be dominated.

The most destructive manifestation of the differing sexual roles for males and females is evident in the violence against women found in "sexual entertainment". Pornography and prostitution exist primarily because there is a male demand for them. There is an unrealistic connotation of glamour attached to the life of prostitutes and women in pornographic films. Yet, the sobering reality is that the great majority of these women work out of economic necessity, and many have suffered sexual abuse as children.

Several recent studies have examined the economics of prostitution. Researchers in Winnipeg discovered that, of 54 prostitutes interviewed, virtually all the respondents cited a need for money as the primary reason for entering prostitution (Elizabeth Fry Society 1985). Most were supporting another adult from their income (77 percent), and over half were supporting dependent children (54 percent). Of equal importance was the fact that a substantial proportion (88 percent) of the prostitutes interviewed reported instances of physical, sexual and verbal/emotional abuse as children. Of this group, nearly 70 percent had specifically experienced physical or sexual abuse. Without exception, those who suffered from sexual abuse recalled the abuser as someone they were close to as opposed to a stranger, with 95 percent of the sexual abusers identified as a blood or legal relative. Only 12 percent reported no abuse as a child.

The Fraser Commission on Pornography and Prostitution also provided some facts on prostitution in Canada. For example, the Vancouver study of prostitution (Lowman 1984) reported that one-third of the prostitutes interviewed had experienced family sexual abuse and more than two-thirds were victims of non-family sexual abuse. Among those who were still active, 84 percent stated that they would leave the profession if an alternative well-paying job were available to them. The Prairie Region component of the study (Lautt 1984) revealed that all the prostitutes cited money as the reason for entering prostitution.

In the Winnipeg study, the prostitutes were asked to identify what they disliked about working on the streets. The most common responses given were not liking the "johns" and the sexual act itself, along with the violence and harassment encountered on the job. Seventy-eight percent had experienced either physical or sexual assaults while one-half had been subjected to both forms of violence since they began prostituting. Almost all the women (94 percent) responded that they drank and used drugs. Their reasons for alcohol and drug use focused primarily on making their lives tolerable. Responses included: "Makes this job a little easier"; "Reality can be dulled"; and, "I can't work unless I'm drunk or high." One woman expressed her feelings in the following way: "It's hard to keep smiling and pretend you're interested in the men you're dealing with. Alcohol and drugs make it easier."

The experiences of women in pornography are similar to those of prostitutes. Personal accounts from women involved in pornography suggest that economic necessity is a definite factor leading to involvement in pornography. Physical and sexual violence are also present in the course of their work (see Lederer 1980; Lovelace 1980). This violence is very often intimated if not actually carried out in the course of producing pornographic material. The progression to pornography can be gradual, beginning with sexually suggestive photos to sexually explicit photos and finally pornographic pictures and films. In fact, the similarities between pornography and prostitution may well be more real than is apparent. One ex-pornographic model summed up the two occupations in the following manner: "A prostitute is just being more honest about what she's doing. A pornography model can fool herself and we did. We called what we were doing 'modeling' or 'acting'. Pornography models have the illusion that they're not hooking. It's called acting instead of sex. Or it's labeled 'simulated sex' – even sometimes when it's not simulated, it's called simulated. But it's all a form of rape because women who are involved in it don't know how to get out" (Lederer 1980, 64).

The condemnation of prostitution and women in such films is not intended to be moralistic or critical of erotica, which portrays consensual sexual relations between adults. Rather, the distinction occurs when these activities become degrading to women. Helen Lagino, in Lederer's book, *Take Back the Night*, provides a concise definition of degrading behaviour: "Behavior that is degrading or abusive includes physical harm or abuse, and physical or psychological coercion. In addition, behavior which ignores or devalues the real interests, desires and experiences of one or more participants in any way is degrading. Finally, that a person has chosen or consented to be harmed, abused or subjected to coercion does not alter the degrading character of such behavior" (1980, 29-30). In other words, prostitution and the depiction of women in films and magazines become destructive when women are degraded and abused for the purpose of entertainment.

On a societal level, violence directed toward women under the guise of enjoyment produces injurious consequences. First, it impedes healthy and equitable relationships between the sexes. It takes from women the human qualities, turning them into objects of sex, devoid of dignity and respect. Second, exposure to violence has been found to facilitate and encourage aggressive behaviour among those who view it.[1] The need to address the abuse of women in prostitution and pornography cannot be ignored. A society which allows this form of degradation cannot be left blameless for the violence directed toward all females in the threat of sexual assault.

1 In the United States the National Institute of Mental Health (1982) reviewed empirical research on the relationship between viewing violence on television and later aggressive behaviour. Donnerstein and Linz (1984) reviewed research on the connection between reading pornography and subsequent aggressive behaviour toward women.

THE INDIVIDUAL'S RESPONSE

As part of the pattern of sex role socialization, women internalize the ideology of sexual assault, which causes them to look for fault within themselves. A woman may question her own behaviour and appearance to assess what she has done to deserve an attack. In many cases, if there is little violence, or if she knows her assailant, a woman may not identify herself as a victim of sexual assault (Clark and Lewis 1977). Since aggression and brutality are commonplace to many women in their relationships, a sexual assault may be just a step further along a continuum of violence.

In contrast, it is not unusual for some men to believe they have been unfairly accused when they overpower women sexually because sexual conquest is part of the patriarchal ideology. Within this context, power and dominance are the key elements. Several researchers studying offenders found no evidence to suggest that men assault because of sexual arousal (Wilson and Nias 1976; Wilson 1978; Groth 1979). As long as women continue to accept responsibility for being assaulted, offenders will continue to rationalize or excuse their own behaviour. Nicholas Groth clearly stated the truth about sexual assault: "...all nonconsenting sexual encounters are assaults" (1979, 2). Only when this statement is fully understood and accepted by those in positions of responsibility in our legal system will assailants be forced to accept responsibility for their acts of aggression.

Since the majority of sexual assaults take place between persons who are, at the very least, acquainted and more often are intimately known to each other, it is misleading to consider that it is the behaviour of females being out alone at night, dressing provocatively, or hitchhiking that causes sexual assaults to occur. Assaults between strangers are comparatively rare and disguise the more subtle and private forms of abuse that are kept hidden. Sexual assault victims are extremely isolated and, rather than seeing themselves in the larger social context, they feel as though they are the only victims in their circumstances. In reality, sexual assault is much more common than official statistics indicate. It must be recognized that the issue to consider is not women's behaviour, but the more pervasive combination of male domination and female submissiveness rooted in the patriarchal structure of society that leads to the violence.

THE LEGAL RESPONSE
The repercussions of differing expectations for male and female behaviour are illustrated in the legal response to sexual assault. In conjunction with societal attitudes, both the law and the criminal justice system emerge as being biased against the victim. There are three legal issues which determine the point at which a sexual assault report may be filtered out of the legal system: consent, corroboration and the character of the victim.

Consent
The notion of consent, in legal terms, refers to resistance. Resistance must be sufficient to prove lack of consent. The determination of nonconsent is essentially a subjective one, resulting in arbitrary decisions being made by members of the criminal justice system. They determine whether or not the resistance offered by the victim is sufficient to cause the attack to be labelled as a sexual assault. Circumstances of attacks differ and each victim will react individually to the incident. Her behaviour cannot

be prescribed by anyone other than herself. In a crisis situation, this may be particularly significant since the ability of an individual to think clearly, make rational decisions or recall details may be impaired. A comparison of the behaviour of victims in other violent crimes underlines the exceptional nature of the consent standard for sexual assault cases. Not only are robbery victims encouraged to comply with their assailants, but research indicates that they usually do not offer any resistance. A study of robbery victims by Conklin (1972) revealed that only one in ten offered resistance either by refusal or force. In sexual assault cases as well, police warn victims not to resist. Yet at the same time, the onus is on the victim to prevent the offence from occurring.

Clark and Lewis contest the appropriateness of the issue of consent: "Only in the case of sexual transactions do we refuse to acknowledge that the relevant issue is the offender's behaviour rather than the victim's state of mind" (1977, 164). The victim is placed in the precarious position of having to prove that her reaction was sufficient to establish nonconsent. The telltale signs of nonconsent then become the physical injuries, even though cases of forced consent in the presence of threats (either verbal or by use of a weapon) are no less intimidating to the victim.

Corroboration
The corroboration requirement, in general, relates to testimony or evidence that is provided by anyone other than the victim of a crime. Such evidence is significant in the successful prosecution of sexual assault cases and refers to evidentiary factors independent of the victim's account of the crime. Corroboration is supplied by the testimony

of witnesses or through circumstantial evidence. The general components of corroborative evidence include the following: the victim's injuries, medical evidence and testimony, the promptness of the complaint to the police (or other witness), the emotional condition of the victim, lack of motive to falsify and the presence of semen or blood on the clothing of the victim and accused. It is noteworthy that more than half of the components mentioned are related to the victim's behaviour and condition. Although questions may be directed at the victim on the corroborative evidence, the basis of the evidence will be given by others: namely, police officers and medical personnel.

The importance of corroborative evidence was underlined by a requirement prior to 1976 that instructed judges to warn juries of the danger in convicting a defendant without any corroborative evidence apart from the victim's testimony. The warning to the jury was required for no other criminal charges. A 1976 Criminal Code amendment abolished the requirement, but until the legislation on sexual assault was revised in 1983, judges continued to have discretion in presenting the cautionary instruction to juries. Although this practice has been discontinued, the credibility of the complainant is still bolstered by corroborative evidence. An illustration of this point is found in a case cited in *Criminal Reports*: "The trial judge accepted the evidence of the girl, which although corroboration was not necessary, was corroborated by the medical evidence of bruises to the right breast" (1984, 40, 284).

Implicit in this notion is the fear that women will make false accusations against innocent men. The motives attributed to fabricated reports include guilt, protection of an innocent party, hatred, revenge, blackmail and notoriety. These assumptions, however, disregard both the victim's apprehension about reporting and the legal rules and methods of investigation which effectively minimize the possibility of deceit.

Character and Status of the Victim

The character and status of the victim is another issue that influences the extent to which a sexual assault is prosecuted. According to Clark and Lewis, "Because rape is a crime against property, its key legal element is the status and character of the victim; that is, the judgment of wrongdoing depends upon the nature of the property in question". They continue: "It is hardly surprising, therefore, that virgins and chaste wives are the most highly protected forms of sexual property within the system, and that these are the women which the law perceived as credible...victims" (1977, 117).

An illustration of such values is expressed by a Winnipeg judge in sentencing a defendant to a lengthier than usual sentence of seven years: "What we have here is a brutal rape with violence on an innocent girl, a 15-year-old virgin. He has probably affected her life for her lifetime" (*Winnipeg Sun* July 1982). The offender was further described as "without merit as a human being". The judge's obvious show of contempt is for the attack on a virgin who is deserving of the court's protection, and he has thereby deemed the offence worthy of extreme punishment. The description of the victim as "innocent" implicitly suggests that if she were not a virgin, she would be less than innocent (perhaps guilty) of her fate. If this were so, what protection would she deserve?

Even with restrictions on the questioning of a victim as to her character and past sexual experiences with other men, certain questions may still be raised. An amendment to the Canadian Criminal Code, effective in 1976, required advance notice in writing for any questions regarding the past sexual conduct of the victim with someone other than the accused. The judge then decided during an *in-camera*[2] hearing whether the evidence was "necessary for a just determination of the case". The major drawback was that the decision on such questioning was left to the discretion of the presiding judge. Consequently, the reform leaves open the possibility of allowing the questioning of each victim. This procedure, while further restricted, continues under the 1983 legislation (see chapter 6).

The double standard in the law which concentrates solely on the character of the victim, as opposed to the actions of the defendant who is being tried, may be further aided by a subconscious adherence of the public at large to a double standard of sexual behaviour for men and women. Gager and Schurr elaborate: "Defense attorneys have routinely benefited from this fact, deliberately introducing questions which they know are not permitted merely to plant suspicion against the victim in the minds of judge and jury. Even if the prosecutor is on his toes and quickly voices objection, sustained by the judge, the damage is done, the victim is made suspect; her 'morality' rather than the accused's behavior becomes a central issue" (1976, 156-57). The unreasonable relationship is drawn between the victim's prior sexual activities, whether factual or intimated by defence counsel, and the likelihood that she would have consented to the offence

2 An in-camera hearing is a private consultation between the judge and legal counsel, which excludes the jury and general public from the courtroom.

in question. Within this context, the perceived character and status of the victim exert considerable influence on the outcome of the charges.

The legal issues that have been examined here indicate that the victim, rather than the defendant, may be put on trial. Carrow states further: "In fact, there is evidence to suggest that rather than allowing false complaints to go to trial, this (trial) process tends to discourage many legitimate complaints" (1980, 175).

The foregoing discussion emphasizes the strength of socialization in contributing to the objectification and secondary status of females. As illustrated, some of the more extreme manifestations of violence against women are seen in pornography, prostitution and sexual assault. The personal and legal responses to sexual assault serve to support the status quo and perpetuate the effects of socialization.

CHAPTER IV

The Response of the Victim

EVERY victim of a sexual assault is faced with the dilemma of disclosure. Should she report the assault? Whom can she trust? Who will believe her? Her decision is based on social factors in which the circumstances and effects of the incident, along with other facets of the her life experience, must be examined. Not all victims react the same way in seemingly similar circumstances. Consequently, how this dilemma is resolved must be determined by factors other than the assault itself.

METHODOLOGY

Access to this sort of information can come only from victims. By using the victim's perception of her victimization as well as her manifest act of disclosure, we believed that we could objectively define the relevant factors that would lead a victim to report the assault to the police. In other words, the victim's description of the assault and her actual response of reporting it to the police or dealing with it in some other way would provide us with subjective data (socialization) and hard data (reporting).

With this intention, we approached Klinic, a Community Health Centre based in Winnipeg. Klinic is the only agency of its kind in the province, serving an urban community of 600,000. The agency's sexual assault program offers 24-hour service, providing information, advocacy, support and counselling to victims, via telephone or personal contact with counsellors.

Initially, our request for access to victims and files was regarded with some concern by the clinical director and other agency personnel. Eventually, after considerable negotiation, Klinic granted access with two stipulations. The first was that the researcher collecting the data undergo a training program by the agency as a sexual assault counsellor. The agency wanted the interviewer to be informed about and sensitive to the issue of sexual assault and to be equipped to deal with potential traumatic effects resulting from an interview. The second requirement was that absolute confidentiality of names and identifying information was to be respected. Once these issues were resolved, the study was approved.

Interviewing did not begin immediately after the training was concluded. Before formulating the questionnaire the researcher needed some experience in the "field" in order to be aware of the types of questions that should be asked. This process, however, took much longer than anticipated. The exposure to women who had undergone every sort of violence imaginable opened up a new world for the naive researcher. Some of the women were recent victims, and of those several turned to the agency immediately after an assault. They called from phone booths and hospitals, or just appeared at Klinic, still in shock following an attack. A large number of victims were "survivors," women who were dealing with assaults from the past, possibly never revealed to anyone before. No longer academic theory and discourse, this was reality – the horrifying details of torture, mutilation and psychological terror suffered by women at the hands of other human beings.

DESCRIPTION OF THE SAMPLE

Most of the 75 victims selected for the study came to Klinic for sexual assault counselling, but some initially contacted the agency for other problems such as depression or suicidal tendencies. These clients were often recognized by crisis workers to be victims of sexual assault and were thus referred to the sexual assault program.

The occupational status of the victims or victims' families ranged from unskilled labour (29 percent) to management and professionals (27 percent), with 35 percent falling between the extremes of the occupational scale. The remaining 9 percent were unemployed or could not be classified by the scale we used (Blishen 1967). This evidence contradicts the popular belief that sexual assault is predominantly associated with low social status. It was found that women with high occupational status were more likely to report an assault than were those with lower status. This was consistent with Bart's findings (1975), which indicated that women with professional occupations tended to report assault more often than did other women. This may be because professional women are more likely to be believed by the police (Clark and Lewis 1977) or because they are likely to be better informed of their rights.

Well over half of the victims (59 percent) were under 19 at the time of the offence. Thirty percent were in their twenties and only 11 percent were over 30. Age distribution was similar in Schram's and Meyer's research (1978; 1979). Brickman et al. (1980) in the Winnipeg Rape Incidence Survey found that more than half of the respondents reported being under 17 at the time of their assaults. The results of this study showed that reporting

increased with age. These findings were also consistent
with those of Bart (1975).

More than three-quarters of the victims in the study
were single when they were assaulted, while 12 percent
were divorced or widowed and 9 percent were married or
living as married. Meyer's findings were identical to these.
Clark and Lewis (1977) indicated that 54 percent of their
sample were single, 17 percent were separated or divorced
and 20 percent were married or living as married. Some
of the differences between the findings of Clark and Lewis
and those of the present study are likely due to the fact
that girls under 14 were not included in their study.

The majority of the sample in this study were
Caucasian women; thirteen percent were Asian, Native In-
dian or Métis. This distribution may not, however, reflect
actual victimization patterns. Kilpatrick, Veronen and
Resick (1979) conducted a study at a rape crisis centre in
South Carolina and found that despite the large Black
population, 61 percent of the respondents were
Caucasian, while only 37 percent were Black. Crisis
centres have typically been staffed by white middle class
women, and poor women or women of other races may be
less likely to seek help from these agencies.

RESULTS

In assessing the social stimuli that would ostensibly influence a victim's decision to report a sexual assault to
the police, several factors were considered: the victim's attribution of blame; the nature of the response of the first
person informed; the background experience of the victim (violence, incest); the relationship between the victim
and the offender; the extent of injury to the victim; the-
amount of resistance by the victim; the victim's attitude

to the police. Each of these factors was used to formulate propositions which could be tested with the data and each will be discussed individually.

Victim's Attribution of Blame
Unlike other crimes, there is a stigma attached to being a victim of a "sexual crime". A victim is often considered responsible for causing the assault by placing herself in a vulnerable situation or by behaving irresponsibly and "asking for it". Historically, women have been delegated the responsibility of controlling men's sexual behaviour as well as their own (Brownmiller 1975). Consequently, women who have been assaulted believe they must be accountable. Child and incest victims are also guilt-ridden. In these cases, an adult in authority uses power to gain compliance. Self-condemnation builds up because these victims can do nothing to stop the activity. Since most victims hold themselves to some extent responsible for being sexually assaulted and since society is known to condemn victims, it is not unlikely that they will refrain from reporting the assault. This leads to the first proposition: *The more blame a victim attributes to herself, the less likely she is to report a sexual assault to the police.*

Our results in Table I (factor 1) show that, of the victims who reported, those who blamed themselves for the assault (31 percent) were less likely to report the incident than were those who felt they shared blame with the offender (48 percent). Victims were most likely to report when they believed the assailant was totally responsible (90 percent). It is instructive to note that almost all respondents (87 percent) believed they were entirely or partly to blame for the offence.

TABLE I
Factors Influencing Victim's Decision to Report Sexual Assault to Police

Factor	Reported to Police		
	Yes (%)	No (%)	(N)
1. Victim's attribution of blame			
self	31	69	(42)
shared	48	52	(23)
assailant	90	10	(10)
2. Nature of response of first person told			
supportive	47	53	(51)
non-supportive	21	79	(19)
3. Violence in victim's background			
yes	41	59	(46)
no	48	52	(29)
4. Previous sexual assault			
yes	36	64	(33)
no	48	52	(40)
5. Victim-offender relationship			
stranger	75	25	(16)
casually known	47	53	(17)
familiarly known	43	57	(14)
family	25	75	(28)
6. Injury to victim			
yes	68	32	(25)
no	32	68	(50)
7. Resistance by victim			
yes	47	53	(34)
no	42	58	(40)
8. Victim's opinion of police			
negative	39	61	(28)
neutral	30	70	(20)
positive	59	41	(27)

As Wilson (1978) indicated in his research, the predominant effects experienced by sexual assault victims were feelings of "degradation, humiliation, and self-incrimination". This was blatantly evident during the interviewing, and the results demonstrate that these feelings did influence reporting behaviour.

One of the victims who did not report being assaulted explained that her boyfriend had been "taking advantage" of her, spending her money and "cheating". She had decided to end the relationship and refused to see him. One night he knocked on the door, pleading for a chance to speak to her. When she unlocked the door, he grabbed her and began tearing at her clothes. As she cried and pleaded, he dragged her into the bedroom, sexually assaulted her and walked out, leaving her on the bed shaken. During the interview, she said, "After he left me, I laid there for a long time, not believing what had happened. I wondered if my blouse had been too revealing or if I had just hurt him so much that he had to hurt me back. Maybe I made him remember being rejected by his mother". At no time did it occur to this woman that the responsibility for the attack should have been solely attributed to the offender.

Another striking example of self-blame was disclosed during an interview with a woman who had responded to a request for directions while walking home from the library one afternoon. A male stopped his car and called out to her, indicating that he was looking for a street that she recognized as being only two blocks away. She walked over to the car to assist him and he pointed a gun at her, ordering her to get into the car. She was blindfolded and taken to a place where she was sexually assaulted and tortured for the next fifteen hours. This assault, obviously an extreme of the media stereotype, was reported directly to the police. The victim, however, maintained that the fault was hers because she "should have known better than to speak to a stranger."

Nature of Response from First Person Informed
Notman and Nadelson (1980) point out that the reaction of significant others is an important aspect of how a victim reacts to an assault. Accordingly, it follows that this is a vital issue when a victim must decide whether or not to make a report. The sexual assault victim has been socialized to feel guilty, regardless of the circumstances of the offence. Vulnerability to these emotions is reinforced by negative attitudes and judgments of those with whom she has an emotional attachment. For instance, husbands may view the assault as a form of adultery, while parents may respond with anger because they feel guilty and helpless for having been unable to protect the victim. Children and incest victims often get no support from their families and are subject to disbelief or accusations. Although a supportive response does not eradicate the humiliation, it can ease the burden of guilt for the victim. If a response reinforces the guilt and shame already felt by most sexual assault victims, it is not likely that an attempt will be made to seek justice from the legal system. This leads to the second proposition: *A victim will more likely report a sexual assault to the police if a supportive response has been given by the first person informed of the attack.*

As shown in Table I (factor 2), of the victims who reported, those who received a supportive response from the first person they told (47 percent) were more likely to report the offence than those who received a nonsupportive response (21 percent). Thus, the support a victim receives initially after an assault is a factor which does influence victim reporting.

One young victim talked about being awakened and assaulted by a stranger while on summer vacation. She had been sleeping with her dog in a tent near her parents' trailer because the trailer was too small to accommodate the family and the dog. Her mother angrily declared that it was her own fault because she had insisted on taking her dog. She was told, "Next time you'll know better!" No report was made in this case by parents or victim.

In another case, a woman decided to seek counselling after several attempts to commit suicide. She recalled her mother walking into her bedroom while her father was in the process of molesting her. The memory she retained was, "My mother started screaming and became hysterical. I always thought I had done something wrong." Subsequent assaults reinforced her guilt.

Many victims who had experienced support and sympathy from the first person they told of an assault said that it helped to diminish some of the guilt they were feeling. One victim described a series of clandestine visits from her stepfather that progressed from sexual touching to intercourse. He had always warned that she would be blamed if anyone found out. She finally decided to run away from home, but before leaving, told her sister about the assaults. To her surprise, she discovered that her sister had also been enduring these violations. They held each other and cried, feeling somewhat relieved that they were not alone. Together they informed their mother and subsequently the police were notified. She said, "It was so important to be believed. I always thought it happened because of something I was doing. I felt dirty and ashamed.

When my sister told me it happened to her, I started to understand."

Background Experience of Victim
Groth has said that "many women have such a low sense of self-worth that they don't feel they can expect to be treated as equal, worthy people" (1979, 81). To the extent that females are socialized in their feminine role as the property of males, they are limited in their view of personal freedom. Some women have been trained to perceive violence as normal and may learn at an early age to submit to being sexually used: "Children who have been sexually abused and children and women who have been raped have their concepts of themselves as sex objects strengthened" (Hirsch 1981, 62). Kinnon reported that previous assaults led to further victimization, predisposing women to feel like they were "damaged goods," making them believe they were "unworthy of respect" (1981, 7). An important part of the socialization of women is interpreting violence and control as normal interaction between males and females. If a woman has always been subjected to physical or sexual abuse, she will be more likely to define an aggressive situation as normal. The expectations and definitions that women have internalized serve to maintain the secrecy surrounding sexual assault. Therefore, it is our expectation that reporting a sexual assault is contingent on factors relating to the individual's experience, which affects her perception of how she defines the assault. The third proposition thus states: *A victim will be less likely to report a sexual assault to the police if she has a history of being subjected to violence.*

We found that victims who had been subjected to past violence were somewhat less likely to report an assault

(Table I, factor 3). Of the women who reported, 41 percent said they had experienced violence in the past, while 48 percent had not. Of those who had suffered previous sexual assaults (Table I, factor 4), 36 percent reported the current offence to the police, compared to 48 percent who had not been sexually assaulted before. The fact that some women have learned to expect aggression or forced sex during their lifetime was evident from the interviews. For these women, a sexual assault was merely another incident along a continuum of violence.

One respondent who had never officially reported an assault told of a series of abusive relationships and sexual assaults throughout her life. When asked about violence in her background, she replied, "Not really. My parents punished me, but they weren't what I would call violent. They used to make me keep hot pepper sauce in my mouth for an hour and they'd hit me with a metal belt. My counsellor said that was violence, but I never had anything to compare it with."

Another woman who dismissed the option of reporting an assault, described a father who was inclined to "blow up" without any warning. "He often beat me with a belt until I was black and blue and several times he cut me with a knife. I never thought that treatment was extraordinary. I thought that was what happened to bad people."

Yet another nonreporting victim described the punishment she and her sisters received for being "bad". "My father used to make us kneel down without shirts and then he hit us across our backs with his razor-strop" (a leather band used by barbers for sharpening razors).

Forty-six victims told of varying degrees of cruelty that they had suffered at the hands of parents, step-parents, etc. The least dramatic were comments such as, "Oh, my parents knocked me around a little" or "My father beat my mother and they both beat me and my brothers."

Among the women who said they were victims of incest, many had never thought about reporting as an option. "I didn't know I had any rights, I was only a kid" or "I never thought of it" were replies often heard.

One of the respondents recalled her experience: "My father used to come into our bedroom at night and point to one of us. That meant it was our turn and we knew what was expected of us. We each tried to sleep farthest from the door because the one closest seemed to get picked most often."

Another woman described being kept a prisoner by her father for twenty years. "My stepmother knew what was happening, but she didn't do anything, so I never told anyone." Still another case involved a second generation, "My grandfather would always come to my bed when I slept there. He used to touch me and masturbate on me. I always felt so badly, but I didn't know what to do."

Research points to the possibility that one in four female children could be subject to some sort of encounter before the age of 14 (Russell 1984) and that about 80 percent of these assaults are committed by a male relative or close family friend (Rush 1980). This early socialization teaches children to accept sexual assault as normal. The results of this study offer some evidence that the acquired self-concept continues long after the incest has ceased.

Relationship Between Victim and Offender
Many sources have indicated that the victim who knows the offender experiences more self-blame than if the attack was perpetrated by a stranger (Brodyaga et al., 1975).

If self-blame is a factor that inhibits women from reporting an assault (proposition 1), then the relationship between the offender and the victim is significant. An attack by a stranger fits the public image of a "real" assault. As the relationship between victim and offender becomes closer, defining the assault as a criminal offence becomes more difficult. Furthermore, interpreting sexual assault as an act of passion, rather than what it is – an expression of power and hostility – shifts the responsibility for the act from the offender to the victim. Depending on whether he is a former lover, friend, acquaintance, stranger, or a family member, the victim of a sexual assault will usually experience varying degrees of reluctance to report. The fourth proposition states: *Police reporting will differ according to the degree of familiarity between a victim and offender, with strangers being reported most often.*

We found that strangers were the most likely to be reported (75 percent), while family members were the least reported (25 percent). See Table I (factor 5) for distribution. Although the smallest percentage of offences reported to the police were committed by family members, they constituted the greatest number of offenders of any of the four relationship categories in the study.

Previous researchers have suggested that sexual assaults by strangers are more likely to be reported because these assaults reflect cultural assumptions and are more readily perceived as authentic by others as well as by the victim herself. One item on the questionnaire asked women why they had decided not to report an assault. Most respondents who knew the offenders did not consider reporting to be a legitimate alternative because the relationships often disguised the culpability of the of-

fenders. As self-blame has been found to inhibit reporting, it follows than an offence is less likely to be reported
if it does not fit the stereotypical notion of what women
themselves have been socialized to believe. Replies such
as, "The police wouldn't care," "I didn't think it was a
police matter," "I didn't think I would be believed," were
typical of the 60 percent who did not report and whose
assailants were categorized as closely related (i.e. familiar
and family). Although research suggests that the most
prevalent type of assaults are those which occur between
people who know each other, they are the most under-
reported (Lott et al. 1982).

Extent of Injury to Victim
Skelton and Burkhart (1980) found that the degree of
force used was an important factor in the decision to
report a rape. A victim who is injured finds it easier to
define the attack according to the "social stereotype" of an
authentic assault, thus acting to diminish guilt. The assumption that a crime of violence must be accompanied
by injuries, communicates the message that if sexual assault is a violent crime and there are no injuries sustained, there must not have been a sexual assault. Therefore, a victim without injury may fear that it will be hope-
less to attempt to prove that a crime took place, and this
is likely to deter her from reporting. The fifth proposition
states: *Police reporting will differ according to the degree
of injury sustained by the victim, with greater injury being
positively related to reporting.*

Table I (factor 6) demonstrates that respondents were
twice as likely to report an assault to the police if they
sustained visible injury (68 percent) than if they suffered
less perceptible harm (32 percent). Notably, of all victims

who were injured (33 percent of the total sample), 68 percent reported the offence.

An assault that results in visible injury conforms to the acceptable social criterion of a violent crime. Therefore, injury may permit a victim to more easily define a sexual assault as an illegal act. As one victim stated, "I didn't think there was any sense in reporting it. I had no injuries...who would believe me?" Another woman said, "I knew it would be my word against his. I wasn't even sure it was a crime."

Amount of Resistance by Victim
Although police generally advise women not to resist an attack in order to avoid serious injury or death, Curtis (1974) has suggested that physical resistance results in less emotional trauma for the victim. Weis and Borges (1973) have proposed an inverse relationship between greater trauma and the likelihood of reporting a sexual assault to the police. This leads to the sixth proposition which states: *Police reporting will differ according to the degree of resistance exhibited by the victim, with greater resistance being positively related to reporting.*

Resistance showed a slight positive correlation to reporting (see Table I, factor 7). Of those victims who did resist, 47 percent reported the offence as compared to 42 percent who did not resist.

Women are expected to protect themselves from sexual assault, but their resistance is often seen as teasing or an expression of a desire to be overcome. In order for resistance to be taken seriously, even by the victims, it might require severe injury and that would seem to encourage reporting.

Additionally, individual definitions of the circumstance must be considered when assessing these findings. For example, one respondent who had taken eight years of instruction in tai kwan do recalled the warning of her instructor: "He told us if we didn't think we could overpower the enemy, we shouldn't try. This guy told me he was trained to kill and I wasn't about to test his ability. So I didn't use what I'd learned and at least I didn't get beaten up or killed." This woman did not report the assault, but justified her compliance by reiterating what the instructor had told her. Assaults by strangers were often accompanied by a threat to kill, and although most of the women did not resist when confronted in this manner, their interpretation of the situation in some cases warranted a report to the police.

Attitude of Victim To Police
According to the literature, the victim's opinion of the police appeared to be a generally accepted factor influencing reporting (Ennis 1967; Robin 1977; Schram 1978; Williams and Holmes 1981; Dean and de Bruyn-Kops 1982). Only one study found little support for concern about police hostility as a factor of nonreporting (Wilson 1978).

During the interviewing for this study, however, it seemed apparent that views toward police did not affect reporting. Rather, other factors seemed far more relevant. In general, when offences conformed to the classic or stereotypical version of a sexual assault, victims were more likely to report regardless of their opinion of police. This was the rationale leading up to the seventh proposition: *Police reporting will not differ according to victims' attitudes to the police.*

In Table I (factor 8) we see that although victims who

had a positive opinion of police reported most often (59 percent), those who did not have a positive opinion reported more often (39 percent) than those who were neutral (30 percent). Our results suggest that even if a victim articulates a negative opinion of police, this does not necessarily preclude a report. Many of the nonreporting victims made positive statements about the police, while others were neutral and still did not report. Conversely, some victims who expressed negative feelings about the police did report.

The research also revealed that the manner in which a victim was treated by the police when she did report a sexual assault had some bearing on her impression of them. If she was treated badly, that was reflected in her attitude to them. Kindness on the part of police almost always resulted in a positive opinion of them. These findings suggest that some of the attitudes toward police may be a consequence of reporting rather than a cause.

SUMMARY

To summarize the findings from this study, we found that victims were more likely to report assaults to the police when: (1) they blamed the assailant; (2) they received a supportive response from the first person they told about the assault; (3) they had not experienced physical or sexual violence in their backgrounds; (4) the attack was perpetrated by a stranger; (5) there were visible injuries; (6) and they resisted vigorously, thus increasing the likelihood of injury.

CHAPTER V

The Response of the Criminal Justice System

UNTIL recently, much of the research concerning sexual assault has focussed either on the characteristics surrounding the offence or on the police handling of the reports (Clark and Lewis 1977; Amir 1971; Gager and Schurr 1976). Our research attempts to expand the focus by examining the response of the criminal justice system from the time a victim has contact with the police to the final disposition of the charges. Consequently, the police, prosecution and court levels were included in the analysis. Specifically, an examination was made of the filtering system whereby reported offences are diverted out of the legal system. Filtering refers to the termination or reduction of sexual assault charges as they proceed through the criminal justice system.

METHODOLOGY

We used police file data to obtain information on reports of rape and attempted rape made to the Winnipeg Police Department for the years 1976 and 1977. The file information was supplemented by interviews with the prosecutors assigned to each of the cases that proceeded beyond the police level. These interviews with crown attornies were used to obtain information on the course of the charges once they reached the crown and court levels. Access to file data at the crown level could not be secured because the files are confidential.

The total number of cases that emerged from the study was 154. For each case there was one victim, and one to five offenders. The victims in all cases were female and in all but one case the offenders were male. The total number of offenders, with the inclusion of multiple offender cases, was 211.

The use of data collected in a single jurisdiction proved to be beneficial in several respects. First, official statistics from national data sources used in research have been criticized for the fact that comparability was often lacking for data from different levels of the criminal justice system (Connidis 1979). However, in the present study the same reports were followed through the system, by charge, from the initial contact of the victim with the police to the final disposition. This allowed us to examine the reasons for case attrition where charges are filtered out of the criminal justice system. By using this procedure, the loss of cases in the analysis was avoided. In addition, the data provided information on any reduction of charges so that information was not lost as a result of the re-classification.

As our previous discussion indicates, data utilized in the present study are not representative of sexual assaults in Winnipeg for the two-year study period. Rather, they are representative of the victims who reported the offence to the police and subsequently had a police file prepared. The use of official statistics is reliable to the extent that it represents a select group of sexual assault victims whose victimization is made known to a police agency.

Nonetheless, the information from the police files, used in perspective, provided an excellent opportunity to examine the official response of the criminal justice system to the reports that began at the law enforcement level. There is a filtering system that operates from the police to the judicial level and determines the final outcome of the charges. Connidis (1979) cautions against research that focuses on only one subsystem such as the police and advocates increased research where the entire criminal justice system is examined.

RESULTS
The filtering system of the rape and attempted rape reports was analysed at three levels: the police, crown and court. Each of the three levels have termination points in filtering. The police level deals with charges until they are handed over to the crown prosecutor's office. The prosecutor level processes the cases up to the preliminary hearing. Finally, the court level begins with the preliminary hearing and ends with the final disposition.

The Police Level
The filtering system is evident from the time a report is made by the victim to the police. The level of the police is the first official stage where reports may be filtered out of the system. Here we classified reports as either proceeding to the office of the prosecution or terminating at the police level. Of the 154 incidents reported, 73 were sent to the prosecutor after the initial screening by the police. Of these, the police classified 68 as founded and left 5 reports unclassified (leaving the designation to the prosecutor's office).

Fifty-three percent of the total did not proceed beyond the police level, involving 58 percent of the reported offenders. A summary of the filtering system at the police level is presented in Table II.

T A B L E II
Summary of the Filtering System of Rape and Attempted Rape
Reports at the Police Level by Case and Number of Offenders, 1976
and 1977

Initial Reports Made to the Police		Number of Cases 154	Number of Offenders 211	
Filtering System at the Police Level	Number	Percent	Number	Percent
Unfounded designation	42	27.3	61	28.9
No formal complaint made by the victim	10	6.5	22	10.4
Victim drops charges	7	4.5	16	7.6
No suspect apprehended	22	14.3	23	10.3
Total filtering out of charges at the police level	81	52.6	122	57.8
Number of charges remaining	73	47.4	89	42.2

Cases were terminated for three major reasons: first, the charged was designated unfounded; secondly, no formal complaint was made by the victim or charges were dropped at the police level; or, thirdly, no suspect was apprehended.

Unfounded Designation
The rationale for an unfounded designation on the part of the police can be either subjective or practical. Sometimes the police simply do not believe that a rape or attempted rape has occurred. Police bias was evident in some of the reports. The following comment by police reflects the skepticism directed toward victims' allegations of sexual

assault: "She had been in the suite for a period of about four or five hours and it is doubtful that any victim would be attractive enough for an assailant to wait for that period of time."

In other cases, the police foresee that the prosecutor will have difficulty in proceeding with the charge. Regardless of the veracity of a particular charge, problems related to the victim or to the evidence can affect the chances of proving in court that a rape has occurred. The police classified one report as unfounded with the following justification: "I do not feel that we will be able to present a case against the accused that will result in a conviction. Consent will be the issue and I do not feel that the complainant will be able to convince a court that she said 'no' in a manner that the accused clearly understood."

We also found that the reaction of the victim to the sexual assault was being evaluated on the basis of stereotypical notions of how victims should react, irrespective of individual differences in dealing with the offence. In one case a police officer commented: "I found her to be extremely composed and rational. She did not show any of the usual emotional trauma one would associate with being a rape victim."

The police, however, should not carry the sole burden for an apparent thwarting of justice at this point. The police must be realistic to a certain extent in foreseeing the reactions and prejudices that may emerge from the prosecutors, judges and juries who will ultimately make the decisions regarding the charges. The police must also give some consideration to the efficiency of the police, crown attorney and court system in deciding whether to retain or to filter out a charge. "As a result, the police are forced to operate as an elaborate screening device, a highly selective filter, through which only the 'best' of even the founded cases proceed" (Clark and Lewis 1977, 59). Consequently, one would expect to find the greatest amount of filtering out of reports at the level of the police. In addition, there are cases where the victim's denial of the offence or apprehension about proceeding with a charge lead to an unfounded designation. The police classified 27 percent of the cases as unfounded. The specific reasons for classifying a case as unfounded was given in all but two instances.

In 5 percent of the cases the police referred specifically to problems with evidence as the basis for an unfounded report. The evidentiary problems concerned lack of evidence, lack of resistance and the drunk or drugged condition of the victim at the time of the offence. Intoxication of the victim, according to the police files, was a factor in six of the reports.

For 10 percent of the cases, a combination of police and victim apprehension about proceeding with a charge led to an unfounded report. The victim, in most cases, was generally uncooperative and apprehensive about proceeding with a report. In one case the victim was legally separated from the offender and in another two cases the offender was the ex-boyfriend of the victim. Three of the victims in this group were referred to as having serious drinking problems while two were referred to as "simple minded" and one as severely retarded.

In 5 percent of the cases the unfounded reports were labelled as false complaints. In five of the reports the victim told the police that the allegation of rape was false. Out of this group, police files contained descriptions of one of the victims as incorrigible, one as a neglected child and one as being involved in a lovers' quarrel. There were three cases where the police classified a false complaint without an actual denial of the offence from the victim. Two of these victims were described as being in need of psychiatric help. An unfounded designation was given by the police on the first interview with the victim in four of the reports, on the second interview for three of the reports and on the third interview for one of the reports.

Finally, in 5 percent of the cases the victim did not initially contact the police. Instead, a family relative or witness made the decision to report the offence to the police. The victims in this group, when contacted by the police, denied that a sexual assault had taken place or refused to speak to the police about the incident. One victim's assault was summed up as follows on a police report after the police attended a hospital and were told by the victim she refused to continue any further: "It appears that the complainant was taken in by a 'smooth' operator and is more ashamed of herself than anything. It appears doubtful that there was any offence of rape here as no threats, violence etc. were used." In all but one of the cases, the report was terminated after the initial interview between the police and the victim.

No Formal Complaint by the Victim/
Victim Drops Charges at the Police Level
The next two types of situation which resulted in the termination of a report at the level of the police were initiated by the victim. In some instances, the victim refuses to make a formal complaint after relating the offence to the police. In other cases, the victim decided to drop charges at the police level before it was handed over to the office of the prosecution. A victim might have changed her mind and decided that she did not want to participate in the

lengthy process required for a criminal prosecution. The probability of reliving the sexual assault while testifying in the courtroom is an effective deterrent to many victims in the initial stages of police action. A victim who refused to attend court stated to police that her report was for police information only, as the offender might commit the offence against someone else again. Fear of testifying and refusal to participate in the judicial system proceedings caused some victims to refuse to make a formal complaint or to drop a complaint. There are also many victims who decide not to report the offence to the police at all and consequently are not represented in the study. As seen in the previous chapter, many of the clients of the sexual assault centre chose not to report.

We found that other victims did not want any police involvement in response to the offence. One victim had not intended to call police but her friend had contacted them. After the victim related the offence to the police she stated she did not want involvement in any legal proceedings and only wanted the offender to leave her alone. She revealed that the offender, who was living with her sister, had also attempted to sexually assault her on a previous occasion. In the present study, 6 percent of the victims refused to make a formal complaint. Further, 4 percent had the charges dropped at the police level before crown involvement.

The reasons given by the victim to the police for refusing to press charges are as follows (with the number of times shown in parentheses): family pressures (2); refusal to testify in court (5); victim did not initially make the report (3); fear of reprisal from the offender (1); victim only wanted stolen items returned (1); and victim decided against any further police action (5). With reference to the final category, the police did not hesitate to make broad assumptions regarding the victim's intentions. One of the victims who decided against further police action and was said to be intoxicated was described in the following way: "It would appear she was upset about being dropped out of the car and using the rape accusation as an excuse to try and get back at the guy. It was quite likely he had attempted some sexual activity; however, upon her refusal she was dropped off. She refused any medical attention."

Non-supportive responses affect the victim's decision either to initiate or to continue with a report. These issues add to the notion of the victim's responsibility, whereby the victimization is minimized in seriousness by the stereotyping that plagues the offence. These factors were found to have considerable impact on the victim's decision to report the offence to the police as determined from the research with victims discussed previously.

No Suspect Apprehended
Finally, we found there are some reports made where the victim wishes to proceed on a sexual assault charge but a failure to apprehend the offender renders further police action impossible. At times, a victim does not get a good enough look at the offender to give the police an adequate description. In other instances, even a thorough description does not suffice; a name or a licence number might be needed in order for the police to apprehend the suspect. The absence of witnesses during the offence further complicates the problem of identifying and apprehending the suspect. In the study, 14 percent of the cases had no suspect(s) identified. Reports of this nature are generally kept on file should any new information concerning the identity of the suspect become available.

Summary
The filtering out of reports at the police level accounted for the termination of 53 percent, or 81, of the cases and 58 percent, or 122, of the offenders' charges in the criminal justice system. Apprehension on the part of the police or the victim about proceeding with a report, in addition to the failure to identify and locate a suspect, emerged as the salient factors in the termination of rape and attempted rape reports at the police level.

The Crown Level
The next official to deal with a report of rape or attempted rape is the crown attorney in the provincial Attorney General's Department. "After a case has been referred to the Crown counsel, it may be proceeded with, withdrawn or the charge originally laid may be altered.... The decisions of prosecutors will reflect the priorities of their office which may not be similar to those of the police" (Griffiths et al. 1980, 53).

As mentioned previously, 47 percent, or 73, of the cases were passed on to the level of the crown from the offences reported during the two year study period, involving 42 percent, or 89, of the offenders. For 2 percent of the reports police were unsure whether they should be classified as founded or unfounded. The reports were given to the crown attorney's office for an opinion as to the correct classification. In such cases, the decision was made by a senior prosecutor in the Attorney General's Department..

The crown classified three of these reports as founded and two as unfounded. The two unfounded reports resulted in the termination of charges for 2 percent of the offenders. Preliminary screening by the crown resulted in

46 percent of the cases being proceeded with, comprising 40 percent of the offenders.

Our results on the initial screening at the crown's office reveal consensus between the police and prosecutors, implying similar priorities at the two levels. In fact, the only cases terminated at the crown level were those left unclassified by the police. The data from this study indicate the adeptness with which the police bring forward cases in terms of "second guessing" their acceptance at the crown level.

For 3 percent, however, the victim was instrumental in a total dismissal of charges after the case had reached the prosecutor's office. In these cases, the victim decided that she did not want to proceed any further with the case. In all cases, this occurred before the preliminary hearing had begun. If the victim refuses to continue with the case, the prosecutor generally has no recourse but to drop the charges for want of prosecution.[1] It would be difficult to conduct a trial without the victim for she is the key witness for the crown's case.

Filtering out of charges at the crown level resulted in 6 percent of the charges being terminated. The percentage of offenders whose charges remained in effect now stands at 37. Although we found the actual filtering out of charges at the crown level was relatively minimal, there were modifications that took place respecting the remaining charges. Included were reclassification of original police charges, the use of concomitant and directly related

---

1 While the prosecutor does have a legal recourse provided for in the Criminal Code (Section 635) to send a victim (in her role as a witness) to jail until she agrees to testify, the use of this method is generally considered to be outweighed by the prospect of an uncooperative victim in the proceedings.

T A B L E III

Summary of the Filtering System of Reports at the Crown Level by the
Number of Offenders

Filtering System at the Crown Level	Number of Offenders	
	Number	Percent
Charges terminated		
a) Crown unfounded	5	2.4
b) Victim withdraws participation before preliminary hearing	7	3.3
Charges plea bargained		
a) Plea bargain charge	7	3.3
b) Plea bargain sentence	3	1.4
TOTAL	22	10.4

additional charges, and the use of plea bargaining on
charge and sentence. The crown, like the police, assess
the chances of success in the court system.

Regardless of the subjective, extra-legal factors such
as the victim's demeanour and the circumstances of the
offence, the crown tries to predict whether a particular
female will be seen as a 'genuine' victim by the judges and
juries who will make the decision at the court level.

Reclassification of Police Charges

At this point the crown attorney is in charge of the reports
and may classify charges according to his or her discretion. Charges may be re-classified to lesser ones, or to al-
ternate charges that are deemed to be more appropriate
for the particular offence involved. We found that initially the prosecutor's office did not dismiss any of the charges altogether, but rather decided to file charges less

serious than the original police classification for 4 percent of the offenders. The study found that three charges of indecent assault on a female, three charges of contributing to juvenile delinquency, two charges of sexual intercourse with a female between fourteen and sixteen years and one charge of break and enter with intent to commit rape were laid as alternatives to the original police charges.

Additional Charges

The prosecutor may also decide to include additional charges apart from the major charge. The information that is contained in the crown report during the filing of charges will serve to accommodate the inclusion of additional charges. The additional charges that are laid can serve two major purposes. A case in which there are foreseeable problems with the evidence or the victim's testimony can often be remedied with the possibility of conviction on one of the lesser additional charges, should the case result in an acquittal for the accused on the major charge at trial. A charge of rape where proof of penetration is uncertain could contain a back-up charge of indecent assault on a female so that acquittal of the major charge leaves open the option of guilt on the latter charge.

The second purpose for the prosecutor is the use of additional charges as a plea bargaining tool (Buckle and Buckle 1977). The problematic case may best be served by a negotiated plea or sentence where conviction is almost certain. Plea bargaining eliminates the need for a trial and the uncertain outcome inherent in court proceedings. There are two types of additional charges that were utilized by the crown for the study period: concomitant offence charges and directly related additional charges.

Our information taken from the police reports indicates that the police listed separate additional offence charges for 6 percent of the offenders apart from the sexual assault charge. These charges comprised robbery or theft, attempted murder, assault, and theft and assault causing bodily harm. The crown acted on only one of the additional charges, that being assault (on a relative of the victim by the offender). For the remaining concomitant offences there were two instances where the crown did not file the robbery or theft charges with the major charges; the rest of the charges were contained in the categories of "no suspect apprehended" and "victim did not make a formal complaint."

Directly related additional charges are those involved in the commission of the sexual assault. Offences that are directly related include forcible confinement and gross indecency. The data reveal that of the 12 percent of offenders who went to trial on the original charge(s) laid by the crown, there were six percent who had directly related additional charges included with the major sexual assault charge. A frequency distribution of directly related additional charges for those offenders whose original crown charge was retained, is presented in Table IV. Further examination of the data from the study period indicate that there were no instances where the accused was acquitted on the major sexual assault trial charge and found guilty of the directly related additional charges. Our findings reveal that conviction resulted for one-half of the applicable 6 percent of the offenders who were found guilty of both the major charge and at least one of the additional charges; the remaining 3 percent of the offenders were either found guilty of the major charge only (2 percent) or

T A B L E IV

Frequency Distribution of Directly-related Additional Charges Included with Original Crown Charges, 1976 and 1977*

Directly-Related Additional Charges	Number of Offenders
Assault causing bodily harm	4
Gross indecency	6
Indecent assault	4
Possession of a dangerous weapon	1
Kidnapping	1
Unlawful confinement	1
Forcible confinement	4

*For some of the offenders there were several additional charges laid. The number of offenders with at least one additional charge was 12.

acquitted on the major charge and the directly-related additional charges (1 percent).

Plea Bargaining

Plea bargaining as a method of disposing of cases can be facilitated by the use of additional charges. The crown is able to secure a conviction without a trial. The defence is able to achieve the dismissal of the major and more serious charge and offer the accused a lower penalty for a less serious charge (Klein 1976; Huemann 1978). The accused may also be offered a pre-determined sentence or sentence range in exchange for a guilty plea to the original charge. In plea bargaining arrangements, the prosecutor and defence counsel confer with each other, and they may reach a mutually satisfactory agreement approved by the defendant that will be subject to judicial approval.

In the present study, 3 percent of the offenders agreed

TABLE V
Plea Bargaining in Relation to Charge that Took Place Before the Commencement of the Preliminary Hearing, 1976 and 1977

Plea Bargain Charge	Original Crown Charge	Number of Offenders
Sexual intercourse with a female between 14-16 years	Rape	1
Contributing to juvenile delinquency	Rape	2
Indecent assault on a female	Rape	1
Indecent assault on a female	Attempted rape	3
TOTAL		7 (3.3%)

to plea bargain for a lesser charge before the preliminary hearing began.[2] The alternative charges that were accepted in exchange for a guilty plea are shown in Table V.

Another 1 percent of the offenders plea bargained for a lighter sentence prior to the preliminary hearing.[3] The charges that were plea bargained on sentence as submitted by the crown and defence counsel are presented in Table VI.

Summary
The filtering system in effect at the crown level resulted in 22, or 10 percent, of the offenders' charges being terminated or disposed of in the criminal justice system. Of

2 Information on the stage at which plea bargaining took place was obtained from personal interviews with the prosecutors who had handled the charges.
3 One of the offenders had two separate charges of rape plea bargained in relation to sentence. The offender is represented as two offenders, reflecting the two separate reports of rape involved.

TABLE VI
Plea Bargaining in Relation to Sentence that Took Place Before the
Commencement of the Preliminary Hearing, 1976 and 1977

Pre-Determined Sentence	Crown Charge	Number of Offenders
5-10 year sentence range		
for charges of rape	Rape	2
1 year sentence	Attempted rape	1
TOTAL		3 (1.4%)

these 22 offenders, 12 had their charges terminated altogether, while 10 were involved in a plea bargain with respect to charge or sentence in exchange for a guilty plea. Sixty-seven offenders, or 32 percent of those charged, remained in the criminal justice system for disposition of their charges.

The Court Level
The next stage, the court, results in the final disposition of charges for those offenders still in the criminal justice system. The full spectrum of the court level can involve a preliminary hearing, a trial, sentencing and an appeal. Charges at the final level can be disposed of in a number of different ways: charges may be dismissed, plea bargained on charge, plea bargained on sentence, retained, or finally, may involve a guilty plea without concessions. The crown continues to be very influential at the court level and may attempt to alter the course of the proceedings at any point. The purpose of the preliminary hearing is to determine whether or not the crown has sufficient evidence to proceed with the charges laid. The judge who

presides over the hearing is responsible for the determination of sufficient evidence. "At the hearing...the judge determines whether a *prima facie* case exists, and thus, whether a trial...is warranted" (McCahill, Meyer and Fischman 1979, 160). The crown prosecutor is responsible for presenting the evidence against the accused. Defence counsel attempts to undermine the validity of the evidence, presented by way of victim cross-examination, on behalf of their client. The preliminary hearing is the testing ground for the defence and, to a lesser extent, the crown in terms of attempting to expose any victim or evidentiary weaknesses.

The initial pre-trial hearing has been aptly referred to as a "fishing expedition" for the defence counsel. Intimidation of the victim by way of irrelevant and personal questioning is by no means ruled out, as it reflects on the victim's credibility. "If the defence can show that the victim is not the kind of person who can be believed, then her claim that she did not consent to this particular act of sexual intercourse will be thrown into question" (Clark and Lewis 1977, 47).

Defence counsel works toward a dismissal of the charges at most, and intimidation of the victim at least. It is crucial that the crown counsel intervene and put forth objections to the harassment of the victim by defence counsel. It is the responsibility of the presiding judge to determine which questions are pertinent; the degree of intimidation to the victim ultimately depends on the particular judge, prompted by crown objections at the preliminary hearing.

The preliminary hearing emerges as the crucial phase of the court level since it affects the charges and all that follows. First, the charges may be dismissed by the judge at the conclusion of the hearing if he or she does not think that the evidence warrants a trial. Second, the crown may assess their chances at trial as poor, based on the victim's performance and evidence presented, and opt for plea bargaining. Finally, the victim may terminate the charges by withdrawing her participation in the proceedings.

A trial will follow the preliminary hearing if the judge has decided that a case exists based on the original charges, or if the crown has laid subsequent charges after an initial judicial dismissal of the original crown charge. The mode of trial may be either by a judge sitting alone or by a judge and a jury. The disposition of charges at the court level is shown in Table VII.

Dismissal of Charges

The dismissal of crown charges at the court level can occur at any time after a preliminary hearing date has been set and can result from decisions made by the various persons involved at this level. Our data from the study period indicate that the victim, the crown psychiatrist, the accused and the judge at the preliminary hearing were instrumental in a dismissal of the crown charges.

The preliminary hearing can be a time of apprehension for the victim. Her fears about testifying at the hearing can lead her to withdraw from the process at this stage. McCahill, Meyer and Fischman attribute this phenomenon to a number of factors: "The lack of preparation or support, the prospect of speaking publicly (often for the first time) about a humiliating experience, and the necessity of confronting the offender may contribute to the high rate of victim absence at the preliminary hearing" (1979, 167).

TABLE VII

The Disposition of the Charges at the Court Level by the Number of Offenders, 1976 and 1977

Disposition of Charges	Number of Offenders Number	Percent
Termination of Charges	8	3.8
Subsequent Charges Laid by the Crown		
a) Plea bargain charge	3	1.4
b) Offender found guilty	6	2.8
c) Offender found not guilty	2	0.9
Original Crown Charges		
a) Plea bargained charge	16	7.6
b) Plea bargained sentence	2	0.9
Original Crown Charges Retained		
a) Offender pled guilty - no concessions	2	0.9
b) Consent committal	2	0.9
c) Offender found guilty - all trial charges	15	7.1
d) Offender found guilty - major charge only	4	1.9
e) Offender found guilty of attempted rape instead of the trial charge of rape	1	0.5
f) Offender acquitted of all charges	6	2.8
TOTAL	67	31.8

At the court level, 2 percent of the offenders had their charges terminated because the victim withdrew her participation in the proceedings. In one instance the victim withdrew once the preliminary hearing was in progress. The remaining offenders had their charges terminated after the victim refused to appear at the trial.

The crown psychiatrist was the major force behind a

dismissal of charges for 2 (or 1 percent) of the offenders. In these cases, the psychiatrist came to the conclusion that the accused was insane and therefore not fit to stand trial. The crown, in light of the psychiatrist's decision, dismissed the charges. The crown and defence counsel then agreed upon a consent committal. This resulted in the accused being kept in custody for mental rehabilitation for a indeterminate period of time. In both cases, the consent committal was agreed upon before the preliminary hearing began; these cases will not be considered as valid dismissals given that a period of detention is involved.

In addition, there was one accused (.5 percent) who had his charge dismissed at the request of his co-accused. The crown accepted the offer in exchange for a guilty plea from the co-accused, against whom more evidence was held. The dismissal of charge for one of the accused occurred before the trial. This case represents the single occasion where a plea bargain was achieved by way of a concession for the co-accused.

Finally we found the judge responsible for the termination of some of the charges at the conclusion of the preliminary hearing. The judge determines whether the charges will be brought to trial or dismissed. The data indicate that the charges for 4 percent of the offenders were determined to contain insufficient evidence and were subsequently dismissed by the judge.The total percentage of offenders whose charges were initially dismissed stands at 9 percent, or 19 offenders.[4]

---

4   Aside from the 13 recorded dismissals, there were 6 accused for whom there was no information available as to when the charges were initially dismissed and whether the victim, the prosecutor or the judge was instrumental in that decision.

The crown, in turn, laid subsequent charges for 6 percent of the accused males who had their original crown charges dismissed. The judge at the preliminary hearing was responsible for the initial dismissal of charges for 5 of the accused. In another case, the victim decided to discontinue with the charges before the preliminary hearing began, whereupon the crown laid a charge of assault causing bodily harm on behalf of the victim's sister against the accused.

For the remaining 3 percent of offenders, there was no information available as to the initial dismissal of charges. Data were available for the outcome of the subsequent charges: 3 percent of the accused were found guilty; 1 percent were found not guilty; 1 percent had their subsequent charges dismissed as the victim withdrew her support before the trial began; and a further 1 percent pled guilty before the trial. The conviction rate from the initial dismissals reveals that of 9 percent, or 19, of the accused who had their original crown charges dismissed, only 4 percent, or 9 of the accused were eventually found guilty by way of a trial or a negotiated plea on the lesser charges. In addition, 1 percent of the accused were dealt with by consent committals.

Retained Charges
Charges filed by the prosecutor were retained for 12 percent of the offenders and were subject to both a preliminary hearing and a trial. Among retained charges, the use of plea bargaining was discussed by legal counsel for just over one-half of the offenders. The prosecutor was instrumental in refusing a guilty plea for roughly 70 percent of those charges. The crown's refusal to accept a guilty plea was most often related to having a "strong case"

against the accused. Charges of rape were applicable to 9 percent of the offenders, with attempted rape charges at 2 percent and contributing to juvenile delinquency at 1 percent. Additional charges at trial were included for 7 percent of the accused. The results at trial are as follows: 3 percent of the accused were acquitted on all charges; 7 percent of the accused were found guilty of the major charge only; and .5 percent of the accused was found guilty of attempted rape instead of the original trial charge of rape.

Our results from the study reveal that few crown charges are retained and result in a trial. Out of the 211 persons originally accused of rape or attempted rape, there were only 26 (12 percent)[5] whose original crown charge(s) reached a trial solution. Further, only 19 (9 percent) of the accused were found guilty of at least the major crown charge at trial.

Plea Bargained Charges
The pervasiveness of plea bargaining has been well documented. Counsel on both sides must assess the characteristics of the offence, the credibility of the victim and the amount of crown evidence and must develop strategies to further their respective goals. Realistically, however, success for either counsel is never assured. Plea bargaining provides a means whereby each can benefit; the crown can obtain an admission of guilt from the accused and the defence can obtain the probability of a less harsh outcome for the accused in terms of charge and/or sentence. The

---

5   Three of the accused went to trial on a reduced crown charge of contributing to juvenile delinquency. The remainder of the charges were either rape or attempted rape.

time and energies required by a trial are spared everyone involved in the court proceedings by a guilty plea, especially where there is reasonable doubt about the chances of success for either the crown or the defence.

The benefits of a negotiated guilty plea in a rape or attempted rape case may be obvious to everyone except the victim, who often may feel that the legal process is working to the offender's advantage. A plea of guilty to a reduced charge will be of a less serious nature in legal terms. The pre-determined sentence will specify a sentence or sentence range that will place length of sentence below the maximum penalty allowable to the offender. The plea bargain emerges as a viable alternative to the accused who may not be willing to face the uncertainty of a trial.

A reduction of charge in exchange for a guilty plea resulted for nearly 6 percent of the offenders at the court level. A reduced charge was accepted for 1 percent of the offenders during the preliminary hearing and for 4 percent of the offenders before the court trial. A frequency distribution of the reduced charges accepted by counsel at the court level is presented in Table VIII.

In addition, 2 percent of the offenders had their charges plea bargained but there was no information available as to when the negotiated plea was obtained.[6] Incorporating the above cases into the group of plea bargained cases at the court level results in nearly 8 percent of the offenders being involved in a guilty plea in exchange for a reduced charge.

---

6 No information was available on the prosecutors who had handled the cases.

T A B L E VIII
Plea Bargaining in Relation to Charge that Took Place from the Time
of the Preliminary Hearing to the Trial, 1976 and 1977

Plea Bargained Charge	Original Crown Charge	When Plea Bargained	Number of Offenders
		During preliminary	
Gross indecency	Rape	hearing	3
Indecent assault	Rape	Before trial	3
Contributing to juvenile delinquency	Rape	Before trial	1
Gross indecency	Rape	Before trial	3
Common assault	Attempted rape	Before trial	1
Indecent assault	Attempted rape	Before trial	1
TOTAL			12 (5.7%)

Plea Bargained Sentence
A total of 1 percent of the offenders were involved in a plea
bargain in relation to sentence. A pre-determined sentence or sentence range was agreed upon by the crown
and defence counsel from the time of the preliminary hearing to the court trial. The sentences agreed upon at the
court level are presented in Table IX.

Offender Pled Guilty – No Concessions
The final route that crown charges may take at the court
level is a plea of guilty by the offender without any concessions in the form of plea bargaining. This applied to 1
percent of the offenders from the study period. Both of the

T A B L E IX
Plea Bargaining in Relation to Sentence that Took Place from the
Time of the Preliminary Hearing to the Trial, 1976 and 1977

Sentence Range	Crown Charges	When Plea Bargained	Number of Offenders
9-18 months	Break and enter with intent to commit rape	During preliminary hearing	1
3-5 years	Rape	Before trial	1
10-12 years	Rape	Before trial	1
TOTAL			3 (1.4%)

offenders agreed to a guilty plea on the rape charge after a preliminary hearing had taken place.

Summary
The filtering system at the court level resulted in nearly 8 percent, or 16, of the accused having their charges terminated either by a dismissal (4 percent) or by an acquittal (4 percent). Twenty-four percent, or 51 of the offenders, were found guilty. Of those persons found guilty, 10 percent were found guilty of reduced charges or had sentences reduced through plea bargaining, 3 percent were found guilty of subsequent charges after an initial dismissal of the original crown charges, 1 percent were involved in a guilty plea to the original crown charges without any plea bargaining concessions, 1 percent were involved in a consent committal, and .5 percent were found guilty of attempted rape instead of the trial charge

of rape. Finally, 9 percent of the accused were found guilty of at least the major crown charges at trial.

Conclusion
The filtering system at the police, crown and court levels resulted in a loss of 150 (71 percent) of the original 211 accused persons. Most were filtered out by the police (58 percent, or 122 offenders), with the crown and court levels following at 6 percent (12 offenders) and 8 percent (16 offenders), respectively. The total percentage of offenders convicted for the two-year period was 29 (61 offenders) and comprised findings of guilt on the original crown charges, reduced charges and plea bargained charges.

Our findings confirm that among those sexual assault charges reported, only a select few proceed through the legal system and result in a finding of guilt. The disparity widens when convictions on the original sexual assault charges are examined. A summary regarding the filtering out of charges is presented in Table X.

DEMOGRAPHICS FROM THE STUDY

The Victim and the Offender
Of the 155 victims who reported offences to the police, the majority were under the age of 30 (86 percent). The largest age category was the 15-19 year range representing 38 percent of the victims, followed by the 20-24 year group at 23 percent. Two-thirds of the victims were single (62 percent), which is to be expected given the relative youth of the majority. The category of cohabitation followed at 14 percent. Occupational status revealed that nearly one-half (49 percent) were students or worked in occupations ranging from waitressing to unskilled labour where no

special training beyond basic schooling was required (21 percent). The victims in the study did not emerge as a particularly criminal group with only 6 percent of them having a criminal record mentioned in their files.

The 211 offenders from the study were, for the most part, young in age. The largest age category was the 20-24 year group (36 percent), followed by the 15-19 and the 25-29 year categories at 24 percent each. Just over 58 percent of the offenders were classified as single, with married (21 percent) and cohabitation (11 percent) categories following in frequency. Unskilled labour was the most common occupation listed for the offender (47 percent) with only 2 percent classified as students. Twenty-four percent of the offenders had criminal records; 6 percent had records for previous sexual offences.

Just over half of the reports (56 percent) involved complete strangers. The next largest group involved offenders who could be identified but were not acquainted with the victim (18 percent). Acquaintances accounted for 10 percent. Nearly 10 percent of the cases involved family friends, boyfriends and relatives.

The Offence

The characteristics of the offence revealed that the reported assaults occurred primarily at night and on the weekend (57 and 56 percent, respectively), and during the spring and fall (41 percent). The majority of the reported offences took place in inner city Winnipeg where most of the hotels, drinking establishments and business offices are concentrated. Assaults in vehicles (29 percent) and at an indoor location (22 percent) were more frequent than those at outdoor locations (16 percent). The majority of the offences were reported by someone other than the vic-

TABLE X
Total Filtering Out of Offenders' Charges

Reduction of Charges	Original Crown Charges N=211	Termination of Charges
	Police level N=211	Police unfounded n=61 Charges dropped by victim n=38 No suspect apprehended n=23
Plea bargained charges n=10	**Crown level** n=89	Victim initiated n=7 Crown unfounded n=5
Plea bargained charges n=21 Guilty at trial on reduced charges n=7	**Court level** n=67	Charges terminated (by victim or judges at preliminary hearing) n=8 Acquittal at trial n=8 not guilty by reason of insanity n=2
	Guilty at trial n=21	
TOTAL n=38 18%	TOTAL n=21 10%	TOTAL n=152 72%

tim(58 percent). While the victim made the initial report in 42 percent of the offences, the next three largest categories were stranger/passerby (17 percent), parent/guardian (14 percent) and friend (8 percent).

Stereotypes Not Supported by Data
Several stereotypes and myths have been dispelled by our examination of the characteristics of the offence. The young, "sexually attractive" female was not the only type of victim, as evidenced by an age range that included the very young (1-9 years of age) and the older victim (40-59 years of age). Likewise, the unmarried offender, while constituting the majority, was not the sole type of perpetrator. Nearly one-third of the offenders were in a cohabiting relationship.

Sexual assault occurred primarily in the spring and fall months as opposed to the thermic notion of crime which asserts that most sexual assaults occur in the hot summer months. Further, a sudden outdoor attack was less frequent than attacks in a vehicle, at an indoor residence (other than that of the victim or the offender) and at the victim's residence. These results are not consistent with many of the inaccurate stereotypes held by the public. Importantly, they serve to provide a more realistic picture of the sexual assaults reported.

CHAPTER VI

The Role of
the Prosecutor

THE role of the prosecutor was highlighted in our examination of the response of the criminal justice system to sexual assault. The considerable discretion of the prosecutor in legal proceedings has been addressed by numerous researchers (Grosman 1970; Chambliss and Seidman 1971; and LaFave 1970). In addition, the involvement of the prosecutor emerged in our research as being substantial, given that the crown has responsibility for the charges in the judicial system up to their final disposition. Consequently, the practices and procedures of the crown were integral in gaining insight into the handling of sexual assault charges.

METHODOLOGY

Prosecutors in the Manitoba Attorney-General's Department who had handled sexual assault cases during the two-year study period were interviewed with respect to their general practices and procedures in prosecuting such cases. In addition, the problematic aspects of legal and societal guidelines concerning sexual assault were investigated.

A profile of the prosecutors revealed that of the eighteen prosecutors interviewed, all but one were male. Their ages ranged from 28 years to 45 years with the average age being 33 years. Ten of the respondents had performed other types of legal work before becoming crown attorneys; seven of them had been in private practice, with the remaining lawyers having done defence work, labour relations and police work, respectively. Eight did not have work experience in other areas of legal work. An examination of years of experience in prosecuting sexual assault cases revealed that 56 percent had up to 5 years experience, with an overall range of 2 to 13 years among the prosecutors interviewed.

RESULTS OF STUDY

The Discretion of the Prosecutor

Background
It has been said that prosecutors have the greatest discretionary powers in the criminal justice system (Reiss 1974). In order to understand discretion in the context of the prosecutor's role, the following definition should be considered: "...a public officer has discretion whenever the effective limits on his power leave him free to make a choice among possible courses of action or inaction" (Davis 1969, 4). Discretion here, according to LaFave, may be "...exercised by doing nothing and may exist without express recognition in law" (1970, 532).

The impact of the prosecutor's discretion on the processing of charges of sexual assault is evident. Because the police must anticipate the decision the crown attorney will make on a charge, the prosecutor has an influence on whether the police decide to lay the charge. At the crown and court levels it is the prosecutor who is responsible for proceding with the charge.

Considerable criticism has arisen over the use of plea bargaining as a necessary component of prosecutorial discretion, rather than from the use of discretion *per se.* Plea bargaining is frequently considered illegitimate, stemming from the motivations involved when the prosecutor exercises this form of discretion. Various explanations for the use of plea bargaining have been put forward. The most frequent explanation is that plea bargaining may serve to reduce a backlog of cases. However, some prosecutors do not agree that case overload is the major determinant for the existence of plea bargaining (Heumann 1978). It may be more appropriate to consider a number of factors that, when combined, explain prosecutorial plea bargaining.

Plea bargaining tends to result from various pressures to which the prosecutor is subject. One of the most significant is the "winner take all" adversarial system where the crown and defence are on opposite sides in a trial, culminating in a finding of innocence or guilt for the defendant. Uncertainty about the outcome of a trial figures strongly in the prosecutor's use of discretion. The prosecutor displays his or her competence and efficiency by way of the conviction rate (Buckle and Buckle 1977; Klein 1976). In this sense, a conviction can be achieved by either a plea bargain or a trial conforming to the adversarial model. The prosecutor's record is commonly based on the gross number of convictions and, should he or she lose too many cases, serious questions of competence may arise. In simple terms, the more trials there are, the greater the potential for an acquittal or the loss of a conviction for the crown.

The unpredictability of juries is also a major incentive for a negotiated plea (Heumann 1978). Most prosecutors have had personal experience with the court veterans' adage that "no case is 100 percent certain one way or the other". The implication is not that the prosecutor will negotiate every case. Rather, knowledge and experience will enable the prosecutor to make realistic predictions of the outcome of a trial and to weigh carefully the advantages of a negotiated plea as opposed to a trial.

Problems with prosecuting a case may also prompt the prosecutor to accept a guilty plea to a lesser charge. The chances of success usually involve the strength of evidence and the credibility of witnesses. One prosecutor in a study by Grosman indicated: "...it may just be a matter of logistics and witnesses don't show up and all you can salvage is a plea to something less. It's the best you can do under the circumstances" (1969, 34).

In addition, the prosecutor may have more influence on the sentence with plea bargaining. If the case goes to trial, the judge may be more familiar with the facts and less inclined to concur with prosecutor's recommended sentence. On the other hand, the sentence given by the judge at a trial may correspond roughly to one which might have been achieved through plea bargaining. In this case, the trial may have a marginal effect on the final disposition and the prosecutor may wonder whether it merited so much time and energy.

The prosecutor must also respond to pressures from the various bodies of the criminal justice system: police, defence counsel, judges and social services personnel. Prosecutorial negotiations require mutual cooperation between the various agencies in the system. The concept of a "community game" is used by Cole in a study of a Washington prosecutor's office: "The participants in the legal system (game) share a common territorial field and collaborate for different and particular ends. They interact on a continuing basis as their responsibilities demand contact with other participants in the process. Thus, the need for cooperation of other participants can have a bearing on the decision to prosecute" (1976, 235).

Pressures may be placed on the prosecutor by other members of the criminal justice system for the use of plea bargaining. Plea bargaining can then serve to facilitate the administrative and professional demands placed upon the various agencies with whom the prosecutor interacts.

In Canada, estimates of guilty pleas from regional studies ranged from a low of 44 percent (Hann 1973) to a high of 69 percent (Friedland 1965). However, Hogarth maintains that a 90 percent plus figure for guilty pleas, similar to figures obtained from U.S. studies, is reflective of the Canadian situation (1974).

Initial Charging Phase
The range of prosecutorial discretion is realized in numerous ways. Initially, when the prosecutor receives a report, the decision is made as to whether prosecution is warranted and on what legal grounds. For a sexual assault charge this involves acceptance of that charge at the crown level and the determination of the charge designation; whether it is proceeded with under the original police classification or on an alternative charge. The next step involves the recording of specific information that will serve to accommodate the charging decision. Overcharging may occur at this point in anticipation of plea bargaining. In fact, the interviews with the prosecutors revealed that a sizeable number of them (44 percent) considered directly related additional charges appropriate for use as a plea bargaining tool in sexual assault cases. One of the respondents went so far as to say: "I initially charge 'heavy' in the hopes that the offender will plead guilty and then

drop the lesser ones to spare the complainant testifying (in court)...if you can get a decent plea for the particular rape involved. "

A further 22 percent of the respondents referred to the use of such additional charges as back-ups should the main charge be dismissed or problematic in terms of proof of its occurrence. One prosecutor summed up the use of additional charges in the following way: "The only rationalization is that you have a sneaking feeling that the offender will be acquitted so you hope that the offender will at least be convicted on one of the additional charges."

Plea Bargaining

The crown may retain the original charge or may negotiate with defence counsel for a reduction of charge or a predetermined sentence in exchange for a guilty plea, instead of having the case go to trial. While, in theory, plea bargaining is subject to judicial approval, LaFave asserts that the judicial practice is to follow the prosecutor's recommendations (1970). The prosecutors interviewed for this study unanimously agreed that judges almost always accepted their plea bargaining recommendation.

When questioned as to their opinion of plea bargaining in their jurisdiction, all prosecutors replied they were in favour of it, with one-half of them advocating that certain changes should be made. The respondents who expressed satisfaction with the existing plea bargaining system most often reported that it allowed for a satisfactory agreement for everyone involved. However, data from the study of the filtering system indicated that a satisfactory agreement primarily involved the defence, offender and the crown. The victim was not consulted during the plea bargaining process for just over 70 percent of the guilty plea arrangements that involved a concession for the offender. Explanations given to victims regarding the acceptance of a guilty plea almost always concerned evidentiary problems with the case.

Among the prosecutors who felt that plea bargaining should be retained but changed, the most common objection voiced was the use of last-minute plea bargaining after the court phase had been arranged or was in progress. The study data revealed that such last-minute plea bargaining occurred for 44 percent of the offenders. One solution offered by several respondents was the institution of stricter guidelines governing the timing of plea bargaining. Another solution involved the use of penalties in the form of a fine or an increased jail sentence for the offender who pleads guilty just before the trial.

Several of the respondents were critical of the secrecy surrounding guilty-plea agreements between defence and crown counsel. Disclosure of the reasons for a plea bargain by both counsel in open court was advocated as a means of accountability of counsel to both the judge and the general public. The use of plea bargaining by junior crown attorneys without consulting senior crown attorneys was also a source of dissatisfaction. None of the respondents favoured the elimination of the existing plea bargaining system altogether. However, one of the prosecutors who favoured changes in the system remarked: "If a backlog of cases would not result from the elimination of plea bargaining, I personally would rather work without it."

Pre-Trial Disclosure
The pre-trial disclosure of the crown's information to

defence counsel, beyond the minimum required by law, is also left to the discretion of the prosecutor. The crown decides whether the disclosure will exceed the minimal requirements. The interview results indicated that 22 percent of the prosecutors allowed only minimal disclosure as their usual procedure, while only one of the respondents indicated that full access to information (including witness statements) was allowed. The majority of the respondents (72 percent) revealed that the disclosure of the particulars of the case, excluding witness statements, was the procedure followed. When asked for the circumstances where minimal disclosure was considered appropriate, the responses included: where harassment of the victim was likely; where the prosecutor had a poor relationship with defence counsel; and where there was a weak case or weak complainant. One prosecutor underlined the importance of the victim being a strong witness in court: "The trial is so dependent on the articulation and the confidence of the victim. So, an ethnic thing enters here. Native girls generally aren't as articulate or as confident."

Court Proceedings
The crown also exerts considerable influence on the amount of bail, if any, that is granted, on the selection of the judge who will hear or try the case and on the calendar dates for the case at any stage of the proceedings. The interview results confirmed that prosecutors believe they exert considerable influence over the areas of bail (78 percent) and calendar dates (89 percent). However, all prosecutors denied they had considerable influence over the selection of the judge who presides over a case. When asked to compare their influence with that of the defence

counsel, the majority of the respondents (72 percent) estimated that they had the same influence or more than the defence counsel in those three areas.

This discussion of prosecutorial discretion has provided a realistic examination of the extent of its use. Professional and administrative demands have emerged as the guiding principles in the discharging of that discretion. It was anticipated that the majority of sexual assault charges from the study period would be dealt with as altered charges (plea bargained or reduced crown charges) as opposed to being retained as original crown charges of rape or attempted rape. The data revealed that the majority of charges accepted by the prosecution and disposed of in court were in fact altered by way of plea bargaining or trial on a reduced charge. The figures from the study indicated that 60 percent of the charges were dealt with as altered charges while 40 percent were dealt with on the original crown charge. The use of plea bargaining was considerable, representing almost one-half of the total charges disposed of in court. With reference to the utility of plea bargaining to prosecutors, one of the respondents made the following remark: "It allows you to have the discretion not to waste valuable court time when it's not appropriate – if the outcome is likely to be negative."

The use of altered charges in sexual assault cases was predominant in both the present study and comparable research. Guilty pleas in sexual assault cases have been documented by several researchers, for example, LaFree, 59 percent (1982), and Galvin and Polk, 71 percent (1983). Further, a study by Williams (1978) revealed that 66 percent of defendants in sexual assault cases were convicted on reduced charges, while the remaining 34 percent were convicted on the original sexual assault charge. Conversely, Williams reported that robbery cases resulted in conviction for 73 percent of those tried on a type of robbery-charge. The legal premise of acquittal should reasonable doubt exist[1] emerges as problematic in sexual assault cases where societal attitudes and legal practice place the onus on the victim. Her character, motives and behaviour, areas beyond the scope of the offence itself, are frequently questioned, something that does not happen for most other offences.

Prosecutorial Practices in Sexual Assault Cases

Interaction Between the Prosecutor and the Victim
The prosecutors were asked how many times the victim was usually interviewed prior to the trial. The majority of the prosecutors (72 percent) indicated that the victim was generally interviewed by them twice before the trial. The remainder replied that the victim was either interviewed once before the trial (22 percent) or more than twice before the trial (6 percent). In addition, the prosecutors revealed that the most intensive interviewing usually took place before the preliminary hearing (72 percent) as opposed to before trial (17 percent), with several of the respondents giving equal weight to the interviewing process before both the preliminary hearing and the trial.

Most of the respondents indicated that there was

---

1   Dean and deBruyn-Kops (1982, 84) indicate that a reasonable doubt on the part of the judge or jury may be based on an evidentiary weakness as opposed to a sincere belief that the accused is innocent of the crime.

usually no one present during the interview other than the prosecutor and the victim (61 percent). The remainder reported that the police officer involved in the case (22 percent) or a victim advocate from a crisis centre (17 percent) was present during the interviewing.

All prosecutors felt that counselling services should be provided for sexual assault victims. When questioned as to which agencies could best deliver the counselling, equal weight was given to professionals (psychologists, social workers) and specially trained volunteers at 50 percent each. Hospital-based programs and a combination of the above-mentioned agencies with law enforcement workers was supported by 11 percent and 6 percent of the respondents, respectively. None of the respondents chose the option of the law enforcement agency handling the counselling independently.

The prosecutors were also questioned about the frequency with which victims withdraw complaints after a suspect has been charged. Most of the respondents (61 percent) estimated that 10 percent or less of the victims withdrew charges. The rest (39 percent) indicated that withdrawal by the victim accounted for 20 to 33 percent, with one of the respondents stating that an estimate was difficult to make. One of the prosecutors noted a difference in charge withdrawal by a victim depending on whether she resides in a rural community in northern Manitoba (80 percent) or Winnipeg (10 percent).

The present study revealed that 13 percent of the victims withdrew their complaints after the police had laid charges, with the result that 27 offenders were filtered out of the criminal justice system after being charged with rape or attempted rape. However, a higher percentage of victims (18 percent) withdrew before charges were laid;

proceedings were terminated either at the instigation of the victim (in 22 cases), or because of apprehension about proceeding on the part of both the victim and the police (in 16 cases).

The prosecutors were asked to identify the major reasons for the victim's withdrawal of a complaint after a suspect has been charged. The majority of the respondents (83 percent) identified the fear of testifying in court as the major reason for the victim's withdrawal after a suspect had been charged, indicating an awareness of the trauma involved in the court phase for the victim. The victim's fear may be either perceived (withdrawing before the preliminary hearing) or real (withdrawing at some point after the preliminary hearing). Nonetheless, since the victim is the main (and usually the only) witness in sexual assault cases, the traumatic effect on the victim must be addressed and remedied in order to improve the prosecution of rape cases.

The reason mentioned next in frequency by the prosecutors was that, in their opinion, the victim did not make a sincere complaint (44 percent). The respondents felt that if the legal system does not filter out a false complaint, the victim might take the initiative and withdraw the complaint. One prosecutor commented: "If the victim is not telling the truth she'll probably withdraw at some point. Thorough investigation methods by police and judicial system ensure that a false complaint is discovered. This assures that innocent accused are not convicted." Perhaps this category is also used for reports by victims who withdraw or disappear without giving an explanation, with the prosecutor assuming that the victim had not told the truth about the assault. This, however, is only an assumption as there are cases where there are no explanations given for the victim's withdrawal from the proceedings.

The remaining factors noted by the prosecutors involved personal reasons, the most frequent of which was fear of reprisal from the offender (28 percent). Pressure on the victim from her family or friends to drop the complaint (22 percent) was considered a major factor in the victim's withdrawal. Acquaintance of the victim with the offender (17 percent) may also be related to the fear of reprisal and pressures from family and friends. Sympathy for the offender (akin to victim responsibility) was noted by 11 percent of the prosecutors. Finally, the fear of being known as a rape victim and wanting to forget the assault were given as single responses.

Apart from the above-mentioned reasons given by the prosecutors for the victim's withdrawal after a suspect has been charged, there is an additional factor that may act as a deterrent. A victim who refuses to testify can legally be charged with contempt of court under the Canadian Criminal Code (Section 635), although this rarely occurs.

Relationship Between the Crown and Police
The prosecutors were questioned about their relationship with the police in handling sexual assault cases. All but one of the respondents considered that the degree of cooperation between the two agencies was excellent. The remaining respondent replied that the degree of cooperation was acceptable. None of the prosecutors felt that the relationship needed improvement. The most common response concerning the favourable relationship was that it was necessary for them to work together to ensure the best results. One prosecutor commented: "We're both playing on the same team. We're both in law enforcement.

The only way that a case can be successfully prosecuted is for full disclosure of its strengths and weaknesses between both agencies."

Another prosecutor underlined the importance of working together in the following way: "The necessity of both [agencies] to determine a rapport with respect to the complainant – to screen out any weak complainants." The degree of cooperation between the two agencies was seen in our research, where the crown initially accepted all the reports designated by the police as founded.

Difficulties in Obtaining a Jury Conviction

The prosecutors were asked what they felt were the two major difficulties they found in getting juries to convict for forcible rape. It is interesting to note that all but one of the respondents interviewed felt that the credibility of the victim was one of the major difficulties. Included in this category, apart from the veracity of the victim's account of the offence, were the character and background of the victim. The importance of the victim's credibility in a jury situation is acknowledged by Chappell: "Because of the necessity to prove force or threat of force and lack of consent, and since the victim is usually the prosecutor's only witness, her credibility becomes extremely salient in influencing the decision of jury members"(1975, 85).

The category which followed in terms of frequency of response was that the corroboration requirements are too strict (39 percent). Since this study was completed, the corroboration requirements have been tempered by the new sexual assault legislation (see our discussion in chapter 8).

Other difficulties noted by prosecutors were: the

presentation of the case is limited (22 percent) and the penalties are too severe (6 percent). The additional response category provided specific examples of victim credibility: the notion that 'good girls' don't get raped and the behaviour and conduct of the victim just before the actual offence. The final response concerned the lapse of time in having the case concluded, which corresponds to the notion that "the heart may soften with the passage of time".

The prosecutors were also queried as to the importance of a number of legal and social factors both in terms of the filing of charges and in obtaining a conviction for rape. The five most important factors in the decision to file charges included three elements that are not necessary components of the offence: physical force, injury to the victim and the relationship between the victim and the suspect. The same three elements emerged among the top five factors for obtaining a conviction, with the addition to a further element that is not a necessary component of the offence – the use of a weapon.

Consequently, the data support the assertion that the greater the amount of force and injury, the greater are the chances that a rape charge will be fully prosecuted. There is evidently a shared social consensus by victims and the judicial system about when a case is likely to be taken seriously. The study of the victim's response clearly indicates that a decision to report an offence to the police is contingent on the same factors that are used to justify prosecution. Thus, not only are these elements likely to encourage entry to the system, they also legitimate the charges for legal proceedings. Aside from the injustice of predetermining the legitimacy of an assault, victims are subject to contradictory messages. While, under the "ac-

ceptable" circumstances of attacks by strangers, victims
are expected to vigorously resist (with possible allowan-
ces for threats with a weapon), they are at the same time
told not to resist in order to avoid severe injury or death.

Average Sentence for Rape
The respondents were asked to give an estimate of the
average sentence actually imposed for forcible rape in
Manitoba. The lowest estimate given was 1.5 years while
the highest estimate given was 5 years. The average estimate was 3.5 years. The mean sentence imposed for forcible rape in our study was 3.2 years. The majority of the
prosecutors interviewed felt that the average sentence imposed was inappropriate in terms of being too lenient for
the offence involved (61 percent).

Criticisms of sentencing by prosecutors revealed the
following information. Some respondents said that rape
is one of the most serious criminal offences and is poten-
tially punishable by life imprisonment (22 percent).
Several of the respondents (17 percent) felt that rapes involving violence should have higher sentences than they
do at present. It was also felt that the emotional damage
to the victim should be reflected in higher sentences (17
percent). The opinion that low sentences are not an effective deterrent to potential offenders (17 percent) was also
cited. A final concern regarding low sentences was that
they are inadequate in terms of punishment of the offender (28 percent).

The remainder of the prosecutors interviewed (39 percent) were of the opinion that the average sentence imposed for rape in Manitoba was appropriate. Several of
the prosecutors referred to sexual assaults without a lot
of violence as either "poor salesmanship" or "over-zealous

seductions". This group of respondents felt that the sentence involved generally corresponded to the type of rape involved.

Major Improvements Needed to Deal with
Sexual Assault
The prosecutors were queried as to the most important improvements needed in dealing with the problem of sexual assault. Once again, they expressed their dissatisfaction with the sentencing in sexual assault cases. Most of the respondents (61 percent) indicated that sentencing improvements were the most important changes needed in dealing with sexual assault. Public education dealing with the realities of the offence as opposed to the stereotypes followed in terms of frequency (50 percent). Improvement in the area of services for better aiding the victim and ultimately leading to a higher rate of reporting, was voiced as a major concern (44 percent).

The next two improvements were concerned with controlling the incidence of sexual assault. These were the treatment and rehabilitation of offenders (39 percent) and the teaching of prevention techniques to potential victims (33 percent). It is curious that the prosecutors ranked victim avoidance techniques closely behind treatment for offenders, given that the latter group are the actual perpetrators of the crime.

Legal reform was ranked rather low at 22 percent. Police investigation techniques and prosecution policies were also considered relatively insignificant (11 and 6 percent, respectively). Finally, the under-reporting of the offence was noted by one of the prosecutors and can be linked to the improvement of victim services and public education.

It would appear that the prosecutors interviewed do not see the criminal justice system as a whole playing a significant role in dealing with the problem of sexual assault. The problems cited least often by the prosecutors concerned legal reform, prosecution policies, police training and police investigative techniques. Although sentencing and victim services were among the major problems listed, there was emphasis on the prevention of sexual assault by way of victim avoidance and offender treatment and rehabilitation. While public education about the realities of the offence was deemed significant, the responsibilities of the legal system in addressing sexual assault were not given comparable consideration. In this sense, the use of the legal system was overlooked in importance by the prosecutors as one of the potential educators of the public.

In the context of the theoretical orientation advocated by the authors, it is noteworthy that respondents have proposed a micro solution to a macro problem. Treating offenders (those few who are convicted) and trying to teach potential victims how not to be victimized suggest "band-aid" solutions to much deeper social/structural problems. The notion propagated by this theme is that the issue is one to be dealt with on an individual, rather than a societal, level. However, as long as males and females are operating from unequal positions, violence will continue to be perpetrated on those who have less power.

CHAPTER VII

The New Sexual Assault Legislation

FEATURES OF THE NEW LAW

IN January 1983, the existing rape law in Canada was replaced by sexual assault legislation. The first and most obvious change is that of the designation of the offence. The former offences of rape, attempted rape, and indecent assault on a female or male have been replaced by the offence of sexual assault. The designation is crucial as it correctly shifts the emphasis from sex to violence. As a result, the necessity of penetration has been replaced by the violence of the entire offence. However, the label of "rape" persists and with it the preoccupation with the connotation of sex as opposed to the violence. A media report from Vancouver (*Winnipeg Free Press*, May 1983), in referring to a man thought to be responsible for numerous sexual assaults and not yet apprehended, stated: "The man plans his ambush in advance...sexually assaults or rapes them after luring them into bush areas". Even four to five years later, media accounts continue to label sexual assaults as rape. A headline reading "Rapid Fire Sex Ruled Rape" actually referred to a case in which the accused was found guilty of sexual assault (*Winnipeg Sun*, Aug. 1987). Confusion as to the new sexual assault legislation is heightened by media accounts which continue to distinguish between sexual assault and rape.

Under the new legislation, either a male or female can be classified as a victim or an offender. This change removes the stigmatization of the "female victim" and replaces it with a more equitable definition that includes either of the sexes. The "degenderizing" of offences, however, applies only to those charges replaced by the new sexual assault law. Charges applying only to females, including sexual intercourse with a female under 14 years, with a female between 14 and 16 years and seduction of female passengers on vessels, still remain in the Criminal Code. In addition, the offences of buggery, gross indecency and incest are still accorded separate status and are dealt with outside of the sexual assault legislation.

Sexual assault contains a three-tiered structure of degrees of assault, and includes sexual assault, sexual assault with threats or bodily harm, and aggravated sexual assault. The categories are delineated by factors such as use of a weapon, threat to a third party, victim injury, the number of offenders and the endangerment of life. The maximum sentences vary from 6 months for simple sexual assault to life imprisonment for aggravated sexual assault, depending upon the severity of the offence. The Criminal Code provisions for sexual assault are given below.

SEXUAL ASSAULT - No Defence
   246.1
   1)Every one who commits a sexual assault is guilty of
   a)an indictable offence and is liable to imprisonment for ten years; or
   b)an offence punishable on summary conviction.
   2)Where an accused is charged with an offence under subsection (1) or section 246.2 or 246.3 in respect of a person under the age of fourteen years, it is not a defence that the complainant consented to the activity that forms the subject-matter of the charge unless the ac-

cused is less than three years older than the complainant. 1980-81-82, c. 125, 19.

SEXUAL ASSAULT WITH A WEAPON, THREATS TO A THIRD PARTY OR CAUSING BODILY HARM

246.2

Everyone who, in committing a sexual assault,

a)carries, uses or threatens to use a weapon or on imitation thereof;

b)threatens to cause bodily harm to a person other than the complainant; or

c)causes bodily harm to the complainant; or

d)is a party to the offence with any other person,

is guilty of an indictable offence and is liable to imprisonment for fourteen years. 1980-81-82,c.125,s.19.

AGGRAVATED SEXUAL ASSAULT - Punishment

246.3

1)Every one commits an aggravated sexual assault who, in committing a sexual assault, wounds, maims, disfigures or endangers the life of the complainant.

2)Every one who commits an aggravated sexual assault is guilty of an indictable offence and is liable to imprisonment for life. 1980-81-82, c. 125, s. 19.

CORROBORATION NOT REQUIRED

246.4

Where an accused is charged with an offence under section 150 (incest), 157 (gross indecency), 246.1 (sexual assault), 246.2 (sexual assault with a weapon, threats to a third party or causing bodily harm) or 246.3 (aggravated sexual assault), no corroboration is required for a conviction and the judge shall not instruct the jury that it is unsafe to find the accused guilty in the absence of corroboration. 1980-81-82, c. 125, s. 19.

The new sexual assault law has now been in effect for over five years since its proclamation in January of 1983. We have examined cases tried under the new legislation and have prepared some recommendations aimed at enabling more effective prosecution of sexual offences. The major areas of the legislation analysed are: the meaning of sexual assault; corroboration and recent complaint; the sexual background of the victim; sexual assault of a spouse; prior relationship; the young victims of sexual assault; and the ban on publication of the victim's identity.

ANALYSIS OF KEY AREAS

The Meaning of Sexual Assault
One of the major problem areas identified in the sexual assault legislation is the lack of a definition that sets the offence apart from non-sexual assault. As it stands, the same necessary elements are applied to both assault and sexual assault. The result is the potential for differing interpretations of the actions that constitute a sexual assault. In other words, when does an assault become a sexual assault and what are the necessary elements that make up the offence? A review of cases prosecuted under the new legislation reveals some of the discrepancies in interpreting actions and applying the legislation.

A decision by the New Brunswick Court of Appeal in *R. v. Chase* held that sexual assault as related in the Criminal Code provisions was restricted to an assault on the sexual organs or genitalia and did not include the touching of a woman's breasts. One of the appeal judges stated: "The problem in this case is that the contact was not with the sexual organs of the victim but with the mammary gland, a secondary sexual characteristic" (1984, 286-87). Further, the grabbing of a woman's breasts was equated with other secondary sexual characteristics such as a man's beard. The appeal judge struck down the original conviction for sexual assault and substituted it with a verdict of guilty of common assault.

Several other appeals of sexual assault convictions were subsequently made which were based on the Chase decision. One such case involved an appeal to the Ontario Court of Appeal in *R. v. Gardynik* (1984) on a sexual assault conviction. The argument was made that the accused's actions of trying to kiss a woman, lying on top of her and biting her breast did not constitute a sexual assault as there was no involvement of the complainant's primary sexual organs. The Ontario Court dismissed the appeal, rejecting the Chase decision, and held that when the primary sexual organs were not involved, it was appropriate to determine all the facts in considering whether a sexual assault had occurred. They decided that the assault being appealed had in fact been appropriately defined at trial as a sexual assault. In October 1987 the Supreme Court of Canada clarified the legislation by stating that the touching of breasts was indeed sexual, and therefore constituted a sexual assault.

Another case, that of *R. v. Cook*, heard in the B.C. Court of Appeal, concerned the accused's appeal on conviction for sexual assault. It was questioned whether the touching of the thighs, stomach and breasts of the victim were applicable elements of the offence of sexual assault or nonsexual assault. The B.C. court also rejected the Chase decision and dismissed the appeal. According to one of the judges who heard the appeal: "I do not propose to offer a definition for sexual assault, where Parliament has declined to do so. But I do not think that the characteristic that turns a simple assault into a sexual assault is solely a matter of anatomy. I think that a real affront to

sexual integrity and sexual dignity may be sufficient"
(1985, 149).

The Cook case also addressed the inappropriateness
of equating the old offences (rape, indecent assault) with
the new sexual assault provisions. One of the judges
remarked that a charge of sexual assault might not sus-
tain a charge of indecent assault and vice versa, citing *R.
v. Burden* (1982) from the B.C. Court of Appeal, in which
an accused was acquitted of indecent assault for sitting
next to the victim on a near-empty bus and putting his
hand on her thigh for five to ten seconds. The accused in
this case was subsequently convicted of common assault
after a crown appeal. The judge from the current case further commented: "I think the assault in the Burden case
might well be characterized as a sexual assault, though
it was not characterized in the Burden case as indecent
assault.... If a light but intentional touching may constitute an assault, then I think that a light but intentional sexual touching may constitute a sexual assault"
(1985, 148).

A further example dealing with the meaning of sexual
assault is the crown appeal of an accused's acquittal on
assault, sexual assault and confinement charges in *R. v.
Taylor* (1985). The charges related to the punishment of
a 16-year-old female on several occasions by a male acting in a role of parental authority. The punishment included taping the victim's hands to a post and pulling her
nightgown up to her neck where she would be forced to
stand for a period of time. On one of these occasions, the
accused used a wooden paddle on the bare buttocks of
the victim while she was so confined. The charges resulted
in an acquittal, as the judge decided the acts did not have
a sexual connotation. It was also concluded that a con-

viction for assault was unwarranted according to Sec. 43 of the Criminal Code which states:

> 43. Every schoolteacher, parent or person standing the place of a parent is justified in using force by way of correction toward a pupil or child, as the case may be, who is under his care, if the force does not exceed what is reasonable under the circumstances.

It was apparently concluded that the punishment given to the victim fell within the parameters of the above Criminal Code provision. The Alberta Court of Appeal rejected the acquittal and ordered a new trial on all the original charges, defining a sexual assault as an act which was intended to degrade or demean another person for sexual gratification, and not restricted only to acts of force involving the sexual organs (1985, 269). The decision further stated that an objective test of whether the actions had sexual or carnal aspects in the opinion of a reasonable observer was sufficient evidence, regardless of the victim's perception of the presence of such sexual aspects.

Definitions for the offence are also needed for setting the parameters as to what reasonably constitutes a sexual assault so as not to unduly trivialize the offence. An illustrative example occurred in the case of *R. v. Thorne* (1985) where an 18-year-old accused was convicted of sexual assault for forcibly kissing the hand of a young female. An appeal by the accused from his conviction to the Ontario Court of Appeal resulted in a verdict of guilty with a conditional discharge. The offence was appropriately classified in appeal court as one without sufficient sexual connotation to be deemed a sexual assault.

The use of the term "rape" lingers on, despite the fact that it no longer applies (legally) to the offence. Since the word can be found in any English dictionary, citing forced sexual intercourse among its meanings, "rape" will undoubtedly persist as the term which is used to define that particular act. However, members of the judiciary and the media have a responsibility to change public perception of the offence by using terms that are consistent with the new law. Otherwise, the power and violence of the assaults will remain trivial in relation to the sexual aspect, thus defeating the motive for changing the law in the first place.

Another problem to consider pertaining to the new term is that it continues to be translated according to the older, more familiar one. This is analogous to the practice utilized by immigrants in attempting to translate a second language by tacitly decoding it through their mother-tongue before uttering their thoughts. Judges, however, are obligated to learn the new "language" and recognize any incongruity. At the trial of *R. v. Daychief* (1985), the judge referred to the term "rape" in sentencing the offender and the decision was appealed. The courts have a particular responsibility not to take any liberties in substituting a legal term with a more familiar or graphic designation. Ignorance of the law cannot be a defence for those who are empowered to apply it. Yet, at the appeal, the original sentence of 13 years was upheld and one of the judges argued:, "...the sentence is to be varied because the judge characterized the offence as 'rape'. It was a rape. That Parliament has chosen to categorize rape and other sexual offences as sexual assault does not change the accuracy of that description applied to this particular assault" (1985, 548).

This is the consequence of what might be called "judicial sclerosis", which hinders the ability of a judge to see things according to a new set of conditions. The inability to be flexible combined with discretionary latitude create structural impediments which may sometimes limit the effectiveness of the new legislation.

Recommendations

1. Upon receiving a related case for consideration, the Supreme Court of Canada should set out the appropriate parameters in terms of the actions and elements which constitute a sexual assault. This will result in less confusion regarding the required elements constituting a sexual assault and will enable more equitable application of the legislation.

2. The Supreme Court should consider and provide clarification in the following areas:

(a) The inclusion of reasonable and appropriate secondary sexual characteristics is to be used in the definition of a sexual assault. The presence of sexual connotation or degradation for the purposes of sexual gratification should be based on a reasonable and objective evaluation not by way of including only primary sexual organs or excluding all secondary sexual characteristics in defining sexual assault.

(b) A sexual assault should not be equated with the former offences of indecent assault or rape in order to be considered valid. The intent of the new legislation was to move away from the previous rigidly defined sexual elements (i.e. penetration of the vagina by a penis) and to focus on the aspect of force.

(c) Parameters must also prevent the inclusion of spontaneous and unintentional incidents in the definition of sexual assault. The charging of persons for acts such as unsolicited hand-kisses or hugs would be appropriately dealt with under the assault section as opposed to sexual assault. Including any and all offences with a remote sexual connotation will only serve to hinder the integrity and effective prosecution of cases under the new legislation.

Corroboration and Recent Complaint
The former requirement for corroborative evidence, such as cuts, bruises, torn clothing, or witnesses to an offence which gave credence to a victim's complaint, has been taken out (Sec. 246.4). Legally, a conviction can now be obtained without additional proof that a complainant's testimony is truthful. Nevertheless, the uncertainty of prosecuting on the basis of one person's word against that of another has implications which are unique to sexual assault cases. Women's (and girls') credibility is still undermined by the traditional view that complaints may be motivated by personal factors such as vengeance or guilt. False accusations are no more likely in cases of sexual assault than in any other cases. Attitudes among the members of the judiciary must change in the wake of the legal reform.

In a similar manner, rules relating to the matter of recent complaint have been repealed (Sec. 246.5). Formerly, it was believed that the victim of a "genuine" sexual assault would complain to someone at the first opportunity. This assumption failed to consider the effect a sexual assault may have on some victims. Embarrassment, ambivalent feelings about reporting a family member or significant other, fear of reprisal, or sheer confusion may cause a delay in responding.

Pertinent to both procedural issues is the following judicial interpretation from the Ontario Supreme Court:

"I permitted the complainant to testify that she caused the police to be called almost immediately after exiting the accused's care. I did not, however, permit her to testify as to what she told the police. I did, however, permit her and the police to testify that she made a statement. I did additionally, permit the other witnesses to describe her emotional condition and her state of dress. As well, a doctor testified to her physical condition a few hours after the alleged assault" (*R. v. Page*, 1984).

It is obvious that the matters of corroboration and recent complaint can be construed in a manner which overrides the original intention of the revised legislation. If evidence such as cited in the above case is emphasized to the extent that it detracts from the importance of the complainant's testimony, it may also be used in its absence to cast serious doubt on her credibility.

Recommendation
1. Corroborative evidence such as visible injuries to the victim and early reporting of the offence should not be used in determining the veracity of the charge, and the absence of these elements should not be interpreted as supporting the innocence of the accused.

Sexual Background of the Victim
The questioning of the victim as to sexual activity with anyone other than the accused has always existed in some form under sexual offences legislation. The first substantive amendments occurred in 1976, at which time the victim could be cross-examined regarding prior sexual conduct but was not compelled to answer. In addition, the accused was not permitted to lead evidence which refuted her testimony. However, once these questions had been

asked the damage was done. In the eyes of the jury, a refusal to respond could very well be interpreted as having something to conceal, without regard to the obvious infringement of the victim's right to have the sexual offence in question the focus of attention.

In an effort to reduce harassment and entrapment of the victim by defence counsel, the 1976 amendments to the Criminal Code placed the following restrictions on such questioning.

(1)reasonable notice must be given to the prosecution with the particulars of the evidence sought to be adduced and,
(2)the judge, after an in-camera hearing would decide whether the exclusion of that evidence would prevent the just determination of an issue of fact in the proceedings, including the credibility of the complainant (Sec. 142.C.C.1976).

While at face value the above provisions appeared to have effectively curtailed the innuendo and surprise "attacks" on victims by way of questioning from defence counsel, the judge was then placed in control of decisions made regarding the admissibility of evidence of prior sexual activity. In effect, while restrictions were placed on the questioning by defence counsel, no such restrictions were placed on the judge in deciding whether the information sought was necessary for a "just determination of the case". It is also noteworthy that while inappropriate defence questions were to be abruptly stopped and stricken from the court record, the statement would have already been made, and the innuendo would have been planted in the minds of the jury members.

A further development concerning the 1976 amendments occurred when the Supreme Court interpreted the 1976 amendments in *Forsythe* v. R. (1980) as referred to by Boyle (1984). The court indicated that the victim was required to testify as a witness at an in-camera hearing and that her evidence could be refuted in evidence led by the accused. This decision not only nullified the new provisions but provided less protection to the victim than did the pre–1976 provisions. At this point it became apparent that victims were not protected from personal questioning of a sexual nature – questioning which had no valid relationship to the offence being tried save conjecture or victim-character assassination for the benefit of the defence's case.

With the advent of the new sexual assault legislation in 1983, the provisions for questioning on the sexual background of the victim were clarified. Parameters were set by which judges could ascertain the validity of such questioning, instead of using their own discretion. The new stipulations read as follows:

246.6 (1) In proceedings in respect of an offence under section 246.1, 246.2 or 246.3, no evidence shall be adduced by or on behalf of the accused concerning the sexual activity of the complainant with any person other than the accused unless:

(a)it is evidence that rebuts evidence of the complainant's sexual activity or absence thereof that was previously adduced by the prosecution;

(b)it is evidence of specific instances of the complainant's sexual activity tending to establish the identity of the person who had sexual contact with the complainant on the occasion set out in the charge; or

(c)it is evidence of sexual activity that took place on the same occasion as the sexual activity that forms the subject-matter of the charge, where that evidence relates to the consent that the accused alleges he believed was given by the complainant.

(2)No evidence is admissible under paragraph (1)(c) unless:

(a)reasonable notice in writing has been given to the prosecutor by or on behalf of the accused of his intention to adduce the evidence together with particulars of the evidence sought to be adduced; (C.C. 1983)

Provision (a) concerns admissibility of evidence of sexual activity of the victim by defence counsel where it has been introduced by the crown. The evidence initially given by the crown may include reference either to the victim's sex life or to the absence of one. Provision (b) basically refers to those instances where the accused asserts that he is not the person who committed the offence. Provision (c) is ambiguous, implicitly reinforcing the myth that if a female says yes to one person then consent to others may be inferred when these acts occur on the same occasion.

The first provision of the restriction (Sec. 246.4(1)(a)) has been subject to several appeal challenges by the accused which have ruled in favour of the crown in compliance with the new provision. The first case, *R. v. Wiseman et al.* from the Ontario District Court (1986), concerned evidence given by the victim at the preliminary hearing that she told the accused to let her up and that she did not think it was right that they should use someone else's home. The accused contended that such evidence amounted to sexual activity which should allow the accused to call evidence in reply. The request by the accused was denied on two grounds: (1) the evidence brought out by the crown at the preliminary hearing does not apply to the provision which relates to trial, while (2) the statements made by the victim did not relate to any statements regarding sexual activity.

Another case, *R. v. Gran* (1984), involved an appeal by the accused on the grounds that the trial judge had erred in disallowing cross-examination of the victim with respect to her allegation that she had been sexually assaulted several months earlier. The trial judge disallowed the appeal because the evidence had not been given during the complainant's examination-in-chief, even though such evidence could be described as being of a sexual nature.

An examination of the cases tried under the new legislation indicates that the sexual background of the victim, while further clarified, continues to be a consideration in sexual assault proceedings. The case of *R. v. J.A.* (1984) concerned the sexual assault of a 16-year-old female by her 22-year-old brother who was acting in the capacity of a parent and sole provider for his mother, three brothers and the sister he assaulted. The female complied out of fear upon orders from her brother. The judge stated his contempt for the breach of trust involved between an adult and child, especially when the offender is in a position of authority over the child. However, the severity of the offence was reduced in the eyes of the judge by the following circumstances:

Although, as I have said, this type of behavior is both socially and morally wrong, such occurrences may not warrant the same harsh sentences imposed by Canadian courts confronted with an incestuous relationship between a father and his daughter or between someone acting in *loco parentis* and a young girl. This also holds true if the sister involved in that incestuous relationship with a brother is not of previously chaste character. I hasten to add that previous sexual experiences encountered by a sister do not allow a brother to take advantage of that, but one must realize that the damage, the physical damage, the psychological trauma may not be the same.

Consequently, the offender was given a suspended sentence and placed on two years' probation.

A case which was appealed to the New Brunswick

Court of Appeal by the crown concerned the sentence
given to two defendants accused of sexual assault (*R. v.
Cormier*, 1985). They were given six months and three
months imprisonment, respectively. The crown argued
that the trial judge had erred in stating that the victim's
reputation and lifestyle reduced the seriousness of the offence without any evidence to indicate that the victim
would consent to the advances of the accused. The sentences were revised by the Appeal Court to four years' and
two years' imprisonment.

Recommendations

1. Discussion of the sexual background (past sexual
activity) of the victim should be prohibited altogether from
sexual assault trials. This information bears no relevance
to the charges at hand and only serves to detract from the
seriousness of the offence being tried. Questioning of the
sexual background of the victim initiated by the defence
counsel, although stricken from the court record upon
crown/judicial objections, should result in charges of
contempt of court for defence counsel. These statements
preclude a fair hearing of the charges and plant
suspicions of the victim's credibility in juries.

2. The onus is on the crown to ensure that the past
sexual background of the victim is kept out of the proceedings by way of quickly voicing objection to any such statements made by defence counsel. The judge cannot be
relied on to monitor any and all statements or innuendo
of past sexual activity. Similarly, the crown is cautioned
against introducing the presence or absence of past
sexual activity for the victim. This will open the door to a
rebuttal from the accused and detract from the real issue,
the sexual assault charge.

Sexual Assault of a Spouse

Husbands (and wives) can now be prosecuted under the new sexual assault legislation, regardless of whether they are living together or apart at the time of the offence. Although this new law shows no discrimination on the basis of sex, it primarily deals with the sexual assault of wives by their husbands. Prior to 1983, a husband did not need his wife's consent to have sexual intercourse with her, and he was protected by law in enforcing his wife's "duty" to succumb to his sexual demands.

Canada's first decision under section 246.8 was heard in March 1983 in Grand Prairie, Alberta. Following a guilty plea from the estranged husband of the victim, the judge stated: "I am of the view, and I believe it is common ground, that the degree of trauma associated with a sexual attack is affected by the relationship, if any, between the parties. And I think it cannot be said that the trauma suffered by the victim is as great where there has been a past history of lawful sexual relations with the accused as it would if she were attacked by a stranger" (*R. v. McDonald*, 1983). The assailant received a one-year prison term and one year's probation.

Our data and several other studies have shown that the majority of sexual assaults occur in the home between persons who are known to each other. The trauma associated with a breach of trust between two persons in this type of offence is considerable and must not be minimized by such misleading statements as the one above.

There have been a few decisions favourable to the victims, but sentences have been relatively short compared to cases of similar circumstances which did not involve spouses. Common to all these cases is the extensive injury to the complainants. This corroborative evidence appears to be necessary in practice even though the legal requirement for corroboration has been removed. None of the cases uncovered in our investigation of the new legislation have disclosed a single spousal sexual assault case heard in a Canadian courtroom in which a complainant did not have corroborative evidence. The following excerpt from a case described in Weekly Criminal Bulletin exemplifies this point: "Moreover, it could not be said that the accused could have had an honest belief in the consent of his wife to sexual intercourse, particularly given the degree of violence prior to the act of sexual intercourse" (R. v. A., 1985). The assailant was convicted and sentenced to one year's imprisonment and two years' probation.

The accused in the following case attacked his estranged wife as she entered her car. A guilty plea resulted in one year in prison plus three on probation: "He drove to another location where his own car was parked and tied her wrists with twine to the steering wheel. He forced her to change into a transparent white dress and garter belt. He then drove to another location, masturbated and tried unsuccessfully to have sexual intercourse with her. He ordered her to pose nude in various positions and invited another man to witness it. The entire episode lasted throughout the night for about eight hours" (R. v. Ryan, 1985).

Sentencing of husbands does not seem to reflect the gravity of their offences. An even more blatant example is illustrated in the following case. The first Manitoba decision concerning the sexual assault of a spouse resulted in a conviction and sentence of six months' imprisonment with one year's probation (R. v. Guiboche, 1983). According to the *Winnipeg Free Press*, the husband: "...pursued and caught her and began punching her in the face. He threw her to the ground and began choking her...then dragged his wife along the ground a short distance, pulled her pants to her knees and had intercourse with her against her will...Medical evidence presented at the trial noted (she)...required eight stitches to close cuts to her nose and mouth" (Sept. 8, 1983).

The second conviction in Manitoba (*R. v. Martens*, 1987) for the sexual assault of a spouse occurred in March 1987. The offender was given a three-month sentence for "sexual assault causing bodily harm", which was mitigated by the offender's wife who sent a letter to the judge asking for leniency. Women's groups and the Manitoba Bar Association criticized the sentence, stating that the consideration of the letter by the judge in court was inappropriate.

It must be emphasized that the first step has been taken by removing spousal immunity from the Criminal Code. Nevertheless judicial attitudes must shift along with the legal revision to portray offences against wives to be as serious as assaults against others. Beliefs about women's masochistic tendencies and men's rights to have obedient wives linger on. Meanwhile women's continued dependence on men and their lengthy socialization to be victims keep them silent.

Sexual and physical abuse of wives is a contradiction of the "ideal" institution of marriage, which has us believing that the home is a sanctuary. There is an abundance of research documenting the extensive physical abuse suffered by wives (for example, Martin 1977; Klein 1981). Sexual abuse often accompanies battering as another form of intimidation and expression of power. Sexual assault of wives has not been considered a crime long enough for society and the victims themselves to perceive it as an offence. Thus, sexual assault will have an even lower incidence of reporting than battering. We are not likely to see any significant change until more cases proceed to trial. The stigma associated with sexual assault is even more demeaning to wives than that of battering because it is less clear that an offence has been committed when battering does not accompany the sexual assault. As more cases are made public with fair objective judgments in favour of women who are sexually assaulted in marital relationships, perhaps we will begin to see how extensive the problem of marital assault is.

Recommendations

1. Low sentences given for cases of spousal sexual assault should be appealed by the crown. The fact that the victim and the offender are or were involved in a marital relationship should not negate the objective realities of the violence of a sexual assault which may or may not involve injury.

2. The reporting of spousal sexual assault will only increase when more cases reach the courtroom and the offence can be viewed as a valid one meriting penalties that are equivalent to those imposed for other assaults.

Prior Relationship

Although the credibility of a complainant can no longer be based on past sexual conduct, in the event of a prior relationship with the accused, prejudices inherent in this scenario are reflected in sentencing. For example, a lenient sentence of 90 days to be served intermittently along with two years' probation was handed down to an offender who had tied up his victim and had intercourse with her against her will. "However, the accused had had a sexual relationship with the woman in the past and there was no injury to the woman" (*R. v. Naqitarvik,* 1985).

Another 90-day sentence with three years' probation was imposed on an accused who forced a woman to commit various sexual acts after she had accepted a motorcycle ride from him. Although the victim tried to fight off her attacker, he threatened and overpowered her. It was stated that the accused and the victim were known to each other (*R. v. Ashbee,* 1985).

Alternately, a sentence of two years (increased to five years on appeal) was imposed on an offender who attacked a woman who was walking down the street. He dragged her into bushes, choked her and had forced sexual intercourse with her. This is as close to the classic stereotype of assault as one could conceive. The difference in attitude between the latter and the former two cases is reflected in the appeal judge's comment: "An assault of this nature involving the grabbing of someone minding their own business, going down a public street, is a most serious offence. It is not to be compared to the social engagement that has gone wrong. It is something which this court takes a very serious view of. The trial judge's sentence was manifestly inadequate" (*R. v. Mitchell,* 1984).

The disparities perceived then, to a great extent, depend on the attitudes of those who are making the assessments (i.e. police, prosecutors, judges, juries) and it is obvious that sexual assaults, although they may be similar in effect, are not treated similarly.

The issue of prior relationship is somewhat related to the spousal immunity clause which was removed from the old legislation. Although prior relationship is not itself directly addressed in the new law, the failure of wives to report their husbands is akin to nonreporting by victims who have previously had relationships with offenders. Since closeness of relationship between victims and offenders correlates with a low incidence of reporting, it is not surprising that the response of the courts continues to reflect the old attitudes which have not been seriously challenged with a significant increase of reporting cases. If husbands are successfully prosecuted for sexually assaulting their wives, this will certainly have an effect on cases in which there was a prior relationship.

Recommendation

1. Criteria used for determining seriousness of sexual assaults need to be standardized in practice, according to the three-tiered structure set out under new legislation. The existence of a prior relationship should not be considered. Nonconsent at the time of the offence is the salient point.

Young Victims of Sexual Assault

Unique obstacles ensue when convictions are sought for sexual assaulters of young children.[1] The corroboration requirement which has been removed from sexual assault may still bear relevance for victims of "tender years", particularly where sworn evidence cannot be obtained from

---

1   In January 1988 Bill C-15 came into effect. The amendments deal specifically with child sexual abuse under the Criminal Code and the Canada Evidence Act. The major provisions include much greater latitude in obtaining evidence from children and the use of videotaped testimony of young victims in court. These changes bring great potential in allowing for the testimony of young sexual abuse victims in criminal proceedings. To date, there have been too few cases to provide any feedback on the impact of Bill C-15.

a young victim. The new corroboration provision, section 246.4, states that the conviction of the accused charged with any of the new sexual assault offences (sections 246.1, 246.2, 246.3) and incest (section 150) will not require corroboration to obtain a conviction and that the judge shall not issue any cautionary warning to the jury in the absence of such evidence. However, as Boyle (1984) points out, the provision is unclear as to whether such an exception is applicable to instances of unsworn testimony. The confusion around the acceptability of young victim's testimony is the result of a contradictory provision in the Criminal Code relating to the testimony of young witnesses. The provision, Section 586, reads:

> No person shall be convicted of an offence upon the unsworn evidence of a child unless the evidence of the child is corroborated in a material particular by evidence that implicates the accused.

The crown is then left in a precarious position regarding the admissibility of the young victim's testimony.

The use of a sworn oath as a requirement for testifying in court is in itself subject to criticism. First, the oath does not guarantee honest testimony. Rather, it is the duty of the legal counsel in court to question witnesses to arrive at the accuracy of the testimony given. In this sense, the oath is more a symbolic gesture than a functional procedure. Second, the oath presumes a respect for the truth and an understanding of the consequences of telling lies.

While the accused has the benefit of safeguards against being falsely convicted for sexual assault via provisions restricting children's testimony, there are no corresponding safeguards for the protection of the young sexual assault victim in the court proceedings. What of the preoccupation surrounding the ability of children to tell the truth and to separate fact from fiction? In fact, children may be more likely to relate events reliably. The relative sophistication of adults in comparison to children may facilitate deceit, whereas the more limited life experiences of the child will diminish this likelihood. Carpenter, who has done research on child victims, relates the following on the possibility of children lying about sexual offences: "There is no evidence in the literature or among the service providers that children are unable to distinguish fact from fantasy in these situations. Of course the younger the child the more unlikely it is that the child would or even could imagine such things, given the detail and accuracy with which children repeat these incidents" (Cited in Rush 1980, 155).

Cases considered under the sexual assault legislation (prior to the introduction of Bill C-15 in January 1988) are illustrative of the problematic aspects for young victims. A sexual assault case from British Columbia, *R. v. Andrew F.* (1985) resulted in an acquittal of a male babysitter for the sexual assault of a five-year-old female child. While medical evidence supported the fact that the child had had sexual intercourse, she could not be sworn as a witness. The veracity of the charge against the accused was questioned, as it was unclear whether the child had actually experienced what she was relating or whether she was remembering prior discussion with her parents, police and others. A determination was made that the young child's testimony was unreliable whereupon the accused was acquitted.

A further example concerned the sexual assault of a child where there was no question that the assault had occurred, although the evidence given by the victim against the accused was considered to be uncorroborated and lacking confirmatory evidence. The court considered the frailties of young children's evidence. The victim was described as being reluctant to testify even though she said she was not embarrassed or intimidated. As a consequence, there was reasonable doubt as to the guilt of the accused and he was acquitted (*R. v. Breckinridge*, 1984).

In *R. v. Bird* from the Ontario County Court in 1984, the accused was acquitted of sexual assault of a ten-year-old female. The only direct evidence against the accused came from the young victim, and there were discrepancies noted in her testimony from the preliminary hearing to the trial. Even though corroboration was no longer necessary under the sexual assault legislation, the court had reasonable doubt as to the accuracy of the accusations made by the victim. It was also noted that the alleged acts of the accused were totally out of character for him.

Conversely, the following two cases are illustrative of convictions secured for sexual assaults on young victims with the help of independent corroborative evidence. The first case, *R. v. R.S.* from the Ontario County Court (1985), involved the sexual assault of a twelve-year-old victim by her stepfather. The court noted that it must be extremely cautious in convicting an accused with only the testimony of a young victim even though the evidence was obtained under oath. However, while corroboration was not necessary, there was independent and substantial corroboration of her evidence.

Similarly, in *R. v. Sarabando* (1985), from the same court, an accused was convicted of sexual assault of a fourteen-year-old involving the fondling and kissing of the

victim against her wishes. While it was mentioned that
the victim did not relate most of the details in her discussion with the police, it was noted that her emotional state
and independent evidence substantiated her claims. As
these cases illustrate, while courts refer to the abolition
of the necessity of corroboration, its use is still regarded
as essential for obtaining a conviction in some circumstances.

Concern for the protection of children from sexual assault, with particular abhorrence reserved for sexual assaults on children by persons in positions of trust or
authority, is commonly stated throughout Canadian
courtrooms. However, the sentences given for convictions
do not generally reflect the professed condemnation of
such actions by adults against children. From our review
of child sexual assault cases we found that low sentencing was a consistent trend.

For example, in *R. v. Smaaslet* (1984; 1985) an accused appealed his sentence of 90 days imprisonment for
the fondling of an eleven-year-old he was babysitting.
While the Court of Appeal expressed concern over
breaches of trust and the protection of children, it
proceeded to determine that the 90-day sentence should
be served intermittently as opposed to consecutively.

Another case involved the trial of a male charged with
sexual intercourse with a female under fourteen. The victim was the ten-year-old child of his common-law wife (*R.
v. Gallant*, Ont. Dist. Ct. 1985). Once again, the court emphasized the seriousness of the violation of the parental
trust and cited it as an aggravating factor. Yet, the court
proceeded to note that there was no physical harm to the
child, the offender was no longer living with the victim's
mother and the offender, while having a criminal record,

had employment. The offender was sentenced to seven months' imprisonment followed by two years' probation.

Another case involved the crown's appeal of a sentence of fifteen months' imprisonment given to a father convicted of sexual assault with a weapon on his fourteen-year-old daughter. (*R. v. Thom*, 1985) The offences included sexual assault and the striking of his daughter with firewood. The Court of Appeal judges saw the sentence as fitting and disallowed the appeal.

A final case concerned charges of sexual assault by a grandfather on his thirteen-year-old granddaughter. Two charges were involved and on one occasion sexual intercourse had occurred. At trial the offender was described as being intoxicated during the offences, having no criminal record and a good employment record. It was also noted that the victim had not suffered any emotional trauma from the offences. The grandfather was given a suspended sentence with probation for two years. A crown appeal on sentence resulted in the determination that nine months' imprisonment with two years' probation was adequate (*R. v. Billie*). Surprisingly, this sentence was deemed appropriate in terms of repugnance for the offences and for general deterrence.

A common theme in many of the above cases is the emotional and physical impact on young victims. The issue of harm to the child is minimized by members of the judiciary by drawing attention to the apparent absence of emotional trauma or physical injury. This contention callously neglects the extensive literature on the lasting and devastating effects of sexual abuse on children (Finkelhor, 1979). During this critical stage of development, children's self-concept is easily transformed so that they learn to see themselves as sexual objects. There is an erosion of trust that takes place, trust that should be inherent between a child and an adult caretaker. Again, the issue of an imbalance of power arises. During our interviews with victims, stories of incestuous experiences, sometimes blocked out of memory for years, always re-emerged, manifested through self-destructiveness, suicide attempts and depression. Children are left with scars, whether or not they are obvious at the time of the abuse.

A final issue affecting young victims of sexual assault is the emotional impact of relating the details of the offence to an array of adults including teachers, social workers, police and lawyers. All these discussions and interviews occur before the trial. If the case reaches the court, the child will also be required to testify in front of a number of adults and be subjected to a cross-examination by defence counsel. The trauma for young children, who may find questioning about sexual offences difficult to understand and even more difficult to discuss, may be intensified when the offender is a parent, relative or family friend.

The terror experienced by young victims during the pre-court phase and the eventual prospect of testifying in court are effective in preventing many of the charges from being tried in a court of law. O'Hara reported that police in Vancouver investigated 85 reports of child sexual assault from October to December 1985 with only 33 cases resulting in charges being laid. A reluctance to proceed by victims or parents saw more than one-half of those charges being discontinued (*Maclean's*, Jan. 1986, 47).

Recommendations
  1. The child victim of sexual assault must be listened

to, must be supported, and above all else must be protected during the legal proceedings as much as is possible without violating the rights of the accused. The inherent distrust of children's evidence must end. The onus is on all those in the criminal justice system, from the police through to the judges in the courtroom, to give children a fair hearing.

2. Evidence given by children promising to tell the truth should be afforded the same weight as sworn evidence. Visual or verbal aids should be acceptable alternatives for children to articulate their ability to distinguish between the truth and lies. The formal sworn testimony process (as it applied prior to Bill C-15) is irrelevant to children who are not equipped to deal with the abstract concepts of truth and lies in isolation from more simplistic, though no less accurate, alternative methods of obtaining sworn testimony.

3. The necessity of corroboration for young victims should be abolished. Although this has been addressed in Bill C-15 by removing the cautionary section in the Criminal Code which warns against unsworn evidence given by young witnesses, there is still uncertainty about the relative weight of unsworn evidence. The corroboration prohibition should apply unequivocally to young victims who promise to tell the truth so that all sexual assault victims would be accorded the same protection under the Criminal Code.

4. The use of videotaped evidence should be allowed for child victims of sexual abuse. Properly conducted videotaped interviews can permit child victims to describe in their own way what occurred. The appropriate use of such interviews should reduce the number of times the young victim must recount the attack to police, crown at-

torneys, medical professionals, social workers and others. The introduction of tapes as courtroom evidence can ease the burden and trauma of providing direct testimony.

5. Sexual assault of children by a parent or relative should be considered as serious a crime as assault by a stranger. Belief in the sanctity and continuity of the family has over-ridden our abhorrance of the crime. A family where the sexual abuse of children is occurring does not deserve special protection; the main focus should be on the well-being of the child in that environment.

6. The offence of incest should be abolished from the Criminal Code. The sexual assault of children by blood relatives should not be accorded special status and should be tried under the new sexual assault provisions. Incest is akin to the former charge of "rape" in that it also requires sexual intercourse as a necessary element. The new legislation considers the the use of force or coersion rather than the sexual nature of the offence. Incest, as it is defined, ignores the blended families found in today's society by differentiating between blood relatives and other persons in positions of trust or authority.

Publication Ban on the Victim's Identity
Section 442(3) of the Criminal Code enforces a mandatory publication ban on the name of a victim. This provision has been held for victims of sexual assault under the new sexual assault legislation. Under the old legislation, the onus was on the crown to initiate the publication ban proceedings. In an Ontario sexual assault case, a newspaper challenged the constitutionality of the ban on the basis of the freedom of the press which is guaranteed by the Charter of Rights and Freedoms (*Canadian Newspapers v. Attorney General for Canada, Ontario*

Lawyers Weekly, February 22, 1985). In February of 1985, the Ontario Court of Appeal held that the ban under section 442(3) was of no force and effect. The publication ban should be left to judicial discretion according to the decision. The judge in the Court of Appeal stated: "However, in an exceptional case where it [publication ban] is not merited, the presiding judge should have an opportunity to refuse to make it." The decision is slated for appeal to the Supreme Court of Canada. The judgment from the Ontario Court of Appeal is viewed as an important one with respect to the new sexual assault legislation which was enacted with the intent of facilitating the reporting of sexual assault. The decision allowing for judicial discretion on the publication of a victim's name may act to discourage victims from reporting an assault.

Recommendation
1. The Supreme Court of Canada should consider the mandatory publication ban on the victim's name in sexual assault cases as a necessary safeguard to encourage increased reporting of sexual assaults in line with the intent of the new sexual assault legislation.

The 1983 Sexual Assault legislation has the potential to constitute a marked improvement over the old rape laws. However, as we have seen, legal reform will not automatically change the system of inequality. Along with government initiatives, new definitions and meanings must be introduced and supported within the legal system. Patriarchal ideology still dominates the thoughts and behaviour of society's inhabitants. The legal system is set up to protect the status quo. Thus, nothing less than a concerted effort from without (through the power structure) and within (through changes in attitudes and practices) will adequately deal with gender inequality.

CHAPTER VIII

Conclusion

ALTHOUGH there are variations in status among women (just as there are with men), all females share some measure of powerlessness in relation to males. Defined in terms of femininity, the prevailing conceptions of what are "appropriate" feminine traits and the relegation of women to the (undervalued) roles of wife and mother are paramount to their status as second class citizens of society. Token recognition of a few women scattered throughout the authority system disguises the glaring resistance most women encounter when they deviate from the norms of mainstream society. Our analysis of sexual assault places violence against females within this context. Most victims of sexual assault experience opposition, both socially and structurally. This opposition appears in the form of "blaming the victim", which is manifested through harsh judgment from others, the victim's self-depreciation and an oftentimes insensitive response from the criminal justice system.

Our research indicates that even when the victim initiates legal proceedings, the majority of perpetrators slip through the cogs in the "wheel of justice". We found that nearly three-quarters of the charges studied were diverted from the legal system and that most of this filtering occurred at the police level. This corresponds to the concern many of the victims initially expressed when they were asked why they did not report an assault – that is, fear of the police not believing them. When we took this expressed concern a step further to consider why they were apprehensive, we found stereotyped beliefs about sexual assault were shared by the victim and members of the criminal justice system. The most frequent reason for the filtering out of charges was an "unfounded" designation by the police. In this regard, it was apparent that the police, in exercising their discretionary power, had to speculate on whether the charges would be accepted at the subsequent crown and court levels. Stereotypical definitions of "genuine" offences are formed in relation to judicial and societal responses which have repeatedly shown considerable indifference toward sexual assaults that do not conform to specific unwritten "guidelines". The degree to which the victim is held responsible depends upon how closely she observed socially prescribed behaviour. The victim who hitchhikes, frequents bars or knows her assailant thus becomes suspect. Our research also demonstrates that victims themselves ascribe to these beliefs under such circumstances.

The extent of self-blame experienced by victims is encountered in the second most frequent reason for the filtering out of charges: the victim withdraws charges. First-hand accounts of specific reasons for the victim's withdrawal were not available from the police files, apart from general fear of police, refusing to enter the legal process, and wanting to forget the assault. However, accounts from the interviews with victims indicate that the factors considered most important by the victim in deciding whether or not to contact the police are more fundamental. Her relationship to the offender, attitudes of others, self-blame and the extent of injury she suffered were the significant variables.

Cases studied at the criminal justice level indicated that roughly 30 percent of charges resulted in convictions. Most of these convictions were based on reduced charges which also carried lesser penalties. Only 10 percent of the convictions pertained to original charges laid by police. There is considerable evidence stemming from both studies which indicates similarities in the data. The victims in each of the studies were predominantly young (19 years and under), unmarried and most were students at the time of the offence. In addition, the information received from victims, that they are more likely to report offences when the offenders are strangers (followed by "general knowledge", "acquaintance" and least often when the offenders are "family friend", "boyfriend" and "relative") was confirmed by the data from the police files. Victims are less able and/or willing to identify someone they are familiar with as having committed a crime against them. For those reports that were made to the police, half were initiated by the victim in both studies. This is consistent with the reported assaults as being more readily defined by the victim as meriting legal action.

As is evident from our research, there is little encouragement for victims to report sexual assaults in the expectation of achieving some sense of justice. However, the current state of underreporting not only exacerbates the problem of dealing effectively with the offence in the legal system, it leaves victims without redress and the perpetrators of the crime unaccountable. The legal system clearly must accept some of the responsibility for improving the circumstances. This can be achieved by handling sexual assault charges based on their own merit as opposed to stereotyping "genuine" offences and classifying "appropriate" charges which only result in the filtering out of the majority of charges.

Eradicating myths about sexual assault is an arduous task in a male-dominated society and the new legislation in and of itself cannot remedy the situation. The law is only as innovative as the individuals who use, interpret, and apply it. If victims do not report, the pervasiveness of the offence remains cloaked in secrecy. As long as the legal system and, indeed, society as a whole retain the traditional beliefs which place the onus of the deed on the victim, she will be discouraged from reporting the offence and entering into the legal process.

The new legislation carries with it many of the same problems which existed under the old rape laws. Our analysis of the cases tried under the new legislation reveal that there is still a preoccupation with victim accountability, which is reflected in the number of acquittals and low sentences. The strength of socialization is once again demonstrated as we discover that the implementation of revised laws does not necessarily coincide with the formulation of new beliefs about the offence. For example, although the corroboration provision was removed, we found, over and over again, the need for proof that the assault took place as the victim indicated. The apprehension of accepting the word of women (and children) for such an accusation is still omnipresent. Although it is known that this phenomenon is exclusive to sexual assault cases, the intellectualized knowledge reflected in the revised laws has not yet been internalized.

The notion of breaking down the old structures and re-establishing new institutions devoid of discrimination is an overwhelming concept. Yet, it would appear that, given the imbalance of male/female power, this idea is the only answer. Affirmative action is one practical method of dealing with institutional discrimination. This translates into increasing the representation of qualified women at the higher levels of the social structure, reflecting their actual proportion of the population. This does not refer to tokenism but is rather an acknowledgement of competence among women. In addition, confronting issues such as reproductive freedom for women, child care support systems and wages and pensions for homemakers are important steps toward equality for women.

Education is one of the most effective means of offering new insight to oppressed groups, as well as their oppressors. Recognition of myths and stereotypes helps to dispel them. This is a challenge to educators in every sphere of society. Efforts of the women's movement toward raising the collective consciousness of society have produced sexual assault centres, sexual harassment policies in the workplace, implementation of programs responding to wife battering and child abuse, human rights legislation, as well as the revised sexual assault legislation. While these innovations have resulted in a degree of awareness and advancement, they must be accompanied by continued strong advocacy to bring about significant changes. Assignment of new meanings must stem from the position that the dependent status of females legitimates the assumption of male authority. The progression from authority to violence is only a matter of degree.

REFERENCES

Abbreviations used in the text

CACSW Canadian Advisory Committee on the Status of Women
MACSW Manitoba Action Committee on the Status of Women
NCW National Council on Welfare

Secondary Sources

Amir, Menachim. 1971. *Patterns in Forcible Rape.* Chicago: University of Chicago Press.

Bart, Pauline. 1975. Rape doesn't end with a kiss.*Viva* 11(9): 39-41, 100-101.

Blishen, Bernard R. 1967. Socio-economic index for occupations in Canada.*Canadian Review of Sociology and Anthropology* 4(1): 41-53.

Boyd, Monica. 1984. *Canadian Attitudes Toward Women: Thirty Years of Change.* Ottawa: Labour Canada.

Boyle, Christine L. 1984. *Sexual Assault.* Toronto: Carswell Co. Ltd.

Brickman, Julie, John Briere, Margaret Ward, Marnie Kalef, Adeena Lungen. 1980. Preliminary report of the Winnipeg Rape Incidence Project; Paper presented at the annual meeting of the Canadian Psychological Association, Quebec City, June.

Brodyaga, Lisa. 1975. *Rape and Its Victims: Report for Citizens, Health Facilities and Criminal Justice Agencies.* Washington, DC: Law Enforcement Assistance Administration, U.S. Government Printing Office.

Brownmiller, Susan. 1975. *Against Our Will: Men, Women and Rape.* New York: Bantam Books.

Buckle, S., and L. Buckle. 1977. *Bargaining For Justice, Case Disposition and Reform in the Criminal Courts.* New York: Praeger Publishers.

Canadian Advisory Council on the Status of Women. 1985a. *Women and Part-Time Work.* Ottawa.
- 1985b. *Women and Work.* Ottawa.

Carrow, Debra. 1980. *Rape: Guidelines for a Community Response, An Executive Summary.* U.S. Department of Justice. Washington, D.C.: Government Printing Office.

Chambliss, William J., and R. Seidman. 1971. *Law, Order and Power.* Reading, MA: Addison-Wesley Publishing Company, Inc.

Chappell, Duncan. 1975. *Forcible Rape: A National Survey of the Response By Prosecutors.* Washington, D.C.: Batelle Law and Justice Study Center.

Clark, Lorenne, and Debra Lewis. 1977. *Rape: The Price of Coercive Sexuality.* Toronto: The Women's Press.

Cole, George F. 1976. The decision to prosecute. *Readings in Criminal Justice,* R.H. Moore, ed. Indianapolis: The Bobbs-Merril Company Inc.

Conklin, John E. 1972. *Robbery and the Criminal Justice System.* Philadelphia: J.B. Lippincott.

Connidis, Ingrid. 1979. Problems in the use of official statistics for criminal justice system research. *Canadian Journal of Criminology* 21(4): 397-415.

Criminal Code. R.S.C. 1970, c.C-34, s.143, as amended 1980-81-82, c.125 s.19.

Curtis, Lynn A. 1974. *Criminal Violence: National Patterns and Behaviour.* Lexington, Mass.: Lexington Books.

Davis, K. 1969. *Discretionary Justice: A Preliminary Inquiry.* Baton Rouge: Louisiana State University Press.

Dean, C. W., and M. deBruyn-Kops. 1982. *The Crime and Consequences of Rape.* Springfield, Ill.: Charles C. Thomas Company.

Donnerstein, E., and Daniel Linz. 1984. Sexual violence in the media: a warning. *Psychology Today* 18 (January): 14-15.

Egan, Patricia, ed. 1985. The Canadian Law List, 1985. Aurora, Ontario: The Canada Law Book Inc.

Elizabeth Fry Society of Manitoba and Y.W.C.A. 1985. Making street connections. Winnipeg: unpublished study.

Ennis, Philip H. 1967. *Criminal Victimization in the United States: A Report of a National Survey.* Chicago: National Opinion Research Center.

Finkelhor, David. 1979. What's wrong with sex between adults and children? ethics and the problem of sexual abuse. *American Journal of Orthopsychiatry* 49(4): 692-97.

Freidland, Martin L. 1965. *Detention Before Trial: A Study of Criminal Cases Tried in Magistrates' Courts.* Toronto: University of Toronto Press.

Gager, Nancy, and C. Schurr. 1976. *Sexual Assault: Confronting Rape in America.* New York: Grossett and Dunlap.

Galvin, Jim, and K. Polk. 1983. Attrition in case processing: is rape unique?*Journal of Research in Crime and Delinquency* 20: 126-54.

Griffiths, C. T., J. Klein and S. Verdun-Jones. 1980. *Criminal Justice in Canada, An Introductory Text.* Vancouver: Butterworth and Company.

Grosman, Brian. 1969. *An Inquiry Into the Exercise of Discretion.* Toronto: The University of Toronto Press.

Grosman, Brian. 1970. The role of the prosecutor in Canada. *The American Journal of Comparative Law* 18: 498-507.

Groth, A. Nicholas. 1979. *Men Who Rape: The Psychology of the Offender.* New York: Plenum Press.

Hann, R.G. 1973. *Decision-Making, The Canadian Criminal Court System: A Systems Analysis.* Vol. II. Toronto: University of Toronto Press.

Heumann, Milton. 1978. *Plea Bargaining: The Experiences of Prosecutors, Judges and Defence Attorneys.* Chicago: University of Chicago Press.

Hirsch, Miriam F. 1981. *Women and Violence.* New York: Van Nostrand Reinhold.

Hogarth, J. 1974. *Studies on Sentencing.* Ottawa: Information Canada.

Kilpatrick, Dean G., Lois J. Veronen and Patrick A. Resick. 1979. The aftermath of rape: recent empirical findings. *American Journal of Orthopsychiatry.* 49(4): 658-69.

Kinnon, Dianne. 1981. *Report on Sexual Assault in Canada.* Ottawa: Canadian Advisory Council on the Status of Women.

Klein, Dorie. 1981. Violence against women: some considerations regarding its causes and its elimination. *Crime and Delinquency* 27(1):64-80.

Klein, John. 1976. *Lets Make a Deal.* New York: D. C. Heath and Company.

LaFave, Wayne R. 1970. The prosecutor's discretion in the United States. *American Journal of Comparative Law* 18: 532-48.

LaFree, Gary D. 1982. Variables affecting guilty pleas and convictions in rape cases: toward a social theory of rape processing.Social Forces 58(3): 833-50.

Lagino, Helen. 1980. Pornography, freedom and oppression: a closer look. *Take Back The Night: Women on Pornography,* L. Lederer, ed. New York: Thomas Morrow.

Lautt, Melanie. A report on prostitution in the prairies.Fraser Commission Report on Pornography and Prostitution. Report No. 9.

Lederer, Laura, ed.. 1980. *Take Back the Night: Women on Pornography.* New York: Thomas Morrow.

Lott, Bernice, Mary Ellen Reilly, and Dale R. Howard. 1982. Sexual assault and harassment: a campus community case study.Signs: Journal of Women in Culture and Society 8(2).

Lovelace, Linda, and M. McGrady. 1980. *Ordeal.* Seacaucus, NJ: Citadel Press.

Lowman, John. 1984. Prostitution in Vancouver: the genesis of a social problem. Fraser Commission Report on Pornography and Prostitution. Report No. 8, Vol. II.

Manitoba Action Committee on the Status of Women. 1984. Presentation to the Fraser Commission on Pornography and Prostitution. Winnipeg, April, 1984.

Manitoba Advisory Council on the Status of Women. 1979. *The Royal Commission Report Ten Years Later.* Winnipeg.
Manitoba Bar Association. 1986. *Headnotes and Footnotes.*

Martin, Del. 1977. *Battered Wives.* New York: Pocketbooks.

McCahill, Thomas, L. Meyer and A. Fischman. 1979. The Aftermath of Rape. Lexington, Mass.: D.C. Heath and Company.

Meyer, Linda Carol. 1979. Rape cases in Philadelphia: court outcome and victim response. Ph.D. Dissertation, University of Pennsylvania, 1979.

National Council on Welfare. 1985. *Poverty Profile.* Ottawa.

Notman, N.T., and C. C. Nadelson. 1980. Psychodynamic and life-stage considerations in the response to rape. *The Rape Crisis Intervention Handbook,* Sharon L. McCombie, ed. New York: Plenum Press.

Ohara, Jane. 1986. The search for solutions to sexual abuse.MacLean's (January 27): 46 47.

Reiss, Albert J., Jr. 1974. Discretionary jusice. *Handbook of Criminology,* D. Glaser, ed. Chicago: Rand McNally College Publishing Co.

Robin, Gerald D. 1977. Forcible rape: institutionalized sexism in the criminal justice system.Crime and Delinquency (April): 136-58.

Rush, Florence. 1980. *The Best Kept Secret: Sexual Abuse of Children.* Englewood Cliffs, NJ: Prentice-Hall, Inc.

Russell, Diana E.H. 1984. *Sexual Exploitation: Rape, Child Sexual Abuse and Workplace Harassment.* Sage Library of Social Research, Vol 155. Beverly Hills, Cal.: Sage Publications Inc.

Ryan, William. 1974. The art of savage discovery: how to blame the victim. *Victimology,* Israel Drapkin and Emilio Viano, eds. Lexington, Mass: D.C. Heath and Co.

Schram, Donna. 1978. Forcible rape. *Final Project Report.* National Institute of Law Enforcement and Criminal Justice. Washington, DC: United States Department of Justice.

Senate Committee on Health, Welfare and Science. 1980. *Child at Risk.* Ottawa: Canadian Government Publishing Centre.

Skelton, Carol, and Barry Burkhart. 1980. Sexual assault: determinants of victim disclosure.Criminal Justice and Behavior7(9):229-36.

Solicitor General of Canada. 1984. *Canadian Urban Victimization Survey.* Ottawa

Stanley, Marily G. 1985. The experience of the rape victim with the criminal justice system prior to Bill C-127. Ottawa: Department of Justice, Policy Planning and Development Branch.

Statistics Canada. 1983. *The Canada Census of 1981.* Ottawa: Supply and Services Canada.

- 1984. *Women in the Work World.*

- 1987. *Issue of Earnings of Men and Women, 1986.* Ottawa.

Supply and Services Canada. 1982. *Images of Women: Task Force on Sex-Role Stereotyping in Broadcast Media.* Ottawa.

Veers, J.E., and D.F. Cousineau. 1980. The heathen Canadians: demographic correlates of nonbelief. Pacific Sociological Review (23): 199-216.

Weis, Kurt, and Sandra S. Borges. 1973. Victimology and rape: the case of the legitimate victim. *Issues in Criminology* 8(2): 71-116.

Williams, Joyce E. and Karen Holmes. 1981. *The Second Assault: Rape and Public Attitudes*. Westport, Conn.: Greenwood Press.

Williams, Kristen M. 1978. *The Prosecution of Sexual Assaults*. Institute for Law and Social Research. Washington, DC: National Institute of Law Enforcement and Criminal Justice.

Wilson, Paul R. 1978. *The Other Side of Rape*. Queensland, Australia: University of Queensland Press.

Wilson, Paul R., and David Nias. 1976. *Love's Mysteries: The Psychology of Sexual Attractiveness*. London: Open Books.

Women and Part-Time Work. Canadian Advisory Council on the Status of Women. June, 1985.

Women and Work. Canadian Advisory Council on the Status of Women. February, 1985.

Women in the Work World. Statistics Canada. September, 1984.

Zwarun, Suzanne. 1985. Chatelaine grades the province on women's issues. *Chatelaine* April: 70-74.

Cases

R. v. A., (1985), 14 W.C.B., (Y.T. Terr. Ct.)
R. v. Andrew F., (1985), 14 W.C.B., (D.C.)
R. v. Ashbee, (1985), 14 W.C.B., (Ont. C.A.)
R. v. Billie, 14 W.C.B., (B.C.C.A.)
R. v. Bird, 13 W.C.B., (Ont. C.C.)
R. v. Breckinridge, 13 W.C.B., (Ont. Dist. Ct.)

R. v. Burden, (1982), (B.C.C.A.)
R. v. Chase, (1984), 40 C.R. (3d), (N.B.C.A.)
R. v. Cook, (1985), 46 C.R. (3d), (B.C.C.A.)
R. v. Cormier, (1985), C.C.L., (N.B.C.A.)
R. v. Daychief, (1985) 6 W.W.R., (Alta. C.A.)
R. v. Forsythe, (See Boyle, 1984)
R. v. Gallant, (1985), 14 W.C.B., (Ont. Dist. Ct.)
R. v. Gardynik, (1984), 42 C.R. (3d), (Ont. C.A.)
R. v. Gran, (1984), 13 W.C.B., (B.C.C.A.)
R. v. Guiboche, (Sept. 9, 1983), Winnipeg Free Press
R. v. J.A., (1984), N.W.T.R., (N.W.T. Terr. Ct.)
R. v. Martens (Feb. 27, 1987), Winnipeg Free Press
R. v. McDonald, (1983) (Alta.)
R. v. Mitchell, (1984), (Alta. C.A.)
R. v. Naqitarvik, (1985), 14 W.C.B., (N.W.T. Terr. Ct.)
R. v. Page, (1984), 40 C.R., (Ont. S.C.)
R. v. R.S., (1985), 13 W.C.B., (Ont. C.C.)
R. v. Ryan, (1985), C.C.L., (B.C.C.A.)
R. v. Sarabando, (1985), 13 W.C.B., (Ont. C.C.)
R. v. Smaaslet, (1985), C.C.L., (B.C.C.A.)
R. v. Taylor, (1985), 40 C.R. (3d) 269, (Alta, C.A.)
R. v. Thom, (1985), 14 W.C.B., (B.C.C.A.)
R. v. Thorne, (1985), 13 W.C.B., (Ont. C.A.)
R. v. Wiseman et al., (1986), 22 C.C.C. (3d)

Index